The
Hidden Power
of F*cking Up

The
Hidden Power
of F*cking Up

THE
TRY GUYS

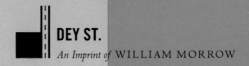

DEY ST.
An Imprint of WILLIAM MORROW

To everyone out there trying

CONTENTS

CHAPTER ONE

Our Failosophy

(and Why Yoda Is Bullshit)

We had to try.

The waves were much higher—and far more frightening—than they were supposed to be. A storm was brewing, and angry clouds gathered on the horizon, inching closer, as the turbulent waves thrashed our dingy life raft like a rag doll. Having already pulled themselves onto the raft, Ned and Eugene lifted Zach from the icy water. Then all three hoisted up Keith. For a moment, it seemed like the crisis was over. And then Keith started vomiting.

Every video has a plan, but this one wasn't going according to ours. Keith, a survival show aficionado, was supposed to "save the day," uniting our fractured family and swooping in during the video's climax to lead our rescue. That was then, this was now, and Keith was lost to us. With each wave he fell deeper and deeper into an abyss of nausea. As the remaining three of us devised a new plan, he continued to heave into the water. The plan to film for six hours was dashed. We needed to get this video done and get our asses back to shore.

That's when we saw the shark.

The more Keith hurled, the more fish gathered to eat it, like chum. Apologies for that image. First came bigger fish, and then the shark. Two of them, actually, both circling curiously beneath us and occasionally piercing the water's surface to see what all the commotion was about. With dorsal fins closing in on our boat, suddenly our "death and dismemberment" insurance paperwork felt very relevant. The plan had totally gone to shit. But we were still there, and our video wasn't about to shoot itself.

With two GoPros and some shitty microphones taped to our chests, we rushed to complete filming before Keith ran out of bodily fluids and the sharks decided to fill the voids in their own empty stomachs. Then we stabbed the bottom of the raft, flooding it, and sunk into the ocean beneath us.

Totally and completely fucking everything up? All in a day's work.

●　　●　　●　　●

In case it wasn't obvious, we're The Try Guys—the lovable quartet best known for our videos in which we, well, try things. From zapping our bellies to simulate the pains of childbirth, to sparring with professional UFC fighters (whose stupid idea was that?), we've done everything in our power to push—nay—annihilate our comfort zones and better understand the people and world around us. Now we're here to pay it forward. Our latest try? This book you're holding (or listening to if you're an audiophile).

But this book is not about succeeding, and it's certainly not about perfection. It's a book about living, about pushing boundaries, and about challenging yourself to reach heights once thought to be impossible. This is a book about embracing failure and riding it on a bumpy but ultimately upward trajectory. Because if our crazy journey has taught us anything, it's that success isn't all it's cracked up to be. In fact, the only way to truly experience all the wonderful, bizarre, satisfying, life-changing, mind-melting, Instagram-doesn't-even-do-it-justice things this world has to offer, is to fail.

In the pages that follow, we're going to share a collection of philosophies that have guided us through making videos and, somewhere along the way, transformed us into better people. We'll also be sharing some stories from our past for the first time ever, carefully handpicked to showcase just how much we've fucked up on our way to becoming the mostly well-adjusted gentlemen you see before you today. Together, we'll all become the best versions of ourselves.

Identifying your insecurities is the first step to self-improvement. Listen, it's okay to not be cool. Believe it or not, we're not cool either; see rest of book. But stick with us here: not being cool *is what makes you cool*. Where most "self-help" books are going to teach you how to be someone else, we're going to teach you how to embrace who you already are. And then we're going to lovingly knock you right out of your comfort zone. Together, we'll reassemble ourselves with the full potential we've always possessed. Watch out world, because the sky's the limit, and even then we can go further.

For most of our young lives, we have zero responsibilities and develop amazing habits like not exercising, eating like crap, never cleaning up after ourselves, and procrastinating whenever given the opportunity (read: always). And then one day, *BAM!*, you wake up and realize your friends have all replaced their movie posters with framed art, the government is asking you to pay something called taxes, and you're just *expected* to know how to cook without burning the house down. But how, though? When did everyone learn how to live? Did we miss some clandestine meeting where everyone discovered the secrets of the universe? If you feel this way, you're not alone. We all do! And it might just get worse before it gets better.

Welcome to life. You're going to fail.

A BRIEF HISTORY OF TRYING

- - - - - - - - -

Everything amazing ever created or accomplished by mankind was forged not via instant greatness, but rather by complete and total failure. Throughout this book we will be sharing some famous, infamous, and downright silly examples of tries throughout history. Hey, if these people never attempted anything scary, we wouldn't be talking about them, would we?

For example, at fifteen, Albert Einstein dropped out of school. A year later, he applied to another school but failed the entrance exam. After that he'd only go on to develop the theory of relativity and be named Time's Person of the Century. Show-off.

We believe failure is the most powerful tool in your arsenal to grow and change and learn. Failure is the building block of everything you want to achieve in life. If "Try New Things" is something we've been told since elementary school, we invite you to *Fail On Purpose*.

Remember "The More You Know," those public service announcements that taught you about the dangers of crack cocaine or dry drowning? We try to live by the opposite credo: *The Less You Know*. You see, the more you *think* you know, the less you want to learn—and learning leads to trying, trying leads to failing, and failing leads to growth. So anytime we think we know it all, we just try to step back and remind ourselves we're idiots. Trust us, this is *good* advice.

The fear of failure is something we've all internalized over the years and it's something we all need to unlearn. Think about how debilitating it is to take standardized tests or audition for a school musical or tell your crush how you feel. You aren't afraid of the action itself—you're afraid of not doing well, of being vulnerable. That's why it's even scarier when you're looking at that cast list or finally get a text back. For a moment, you're powerless to the whims of the world. But we move past it. And when failure motivates us to do better, that's when we really succeed. It's only when failure scares us away from trying again that we've truly been beaten. We have to work to change our perspective: failure is a step forward, not a step back.

It's helpful to remember that some of the greatest writers, thinkers, athletes, and musicians of our day are not special in any way whatsoever, except that they learned how to fail and get back up again. No one is born great. Have you seen babies? They can't even hold pencils, those dummies. Greatness isn't something ordained—it's something you work your ass off for, despite failing over and over again.

Listen, we love Yoda. He's inspirational, he's green. He's like a woke Kermit the Frog. But Yoda's most famous advice was "Do or do not, there is no try." Sorry, but this is complete and total BS. (As is the idea that Luke can become a Jedi Master after only training for a few days, but that's another story.) *Trying is everything!* You can't do without try! You'll never get anywhere without try! No wonder that dude lived alone in a swamp.

That is what this book is about: trying as a form of succeeding, so that you never end up living alone in a swamp like that bastard Yoda.

Wait, Who the Hell Are We?

Why are you listening to us in the first place? Well, we are experts in trying. I mean, it's right there in our name. But, spoiler alert, we weren't always The Try Guys. We didn't emerge from the womb as fully formed viral sensations. (That would have been painful for our mothers.) In fact, becoming the tour de forces (or is it tours de force?) on the internet we are today took a lot of time, a lot of hard work, and the appropriate amount of luck. Before we were The Try Guys, we were just, well, guys with a lowercase *g*. We're so excited to meet you! This is our story.

KEITH HABERSBERGER:
Clown Prince of Tennessee

 **HOWDY, READERS!** This probably sounds weird to say, and I've never told this to the other guys, but growing up in Tennessee I was really blessed to have people be *very* supportive of me . . . to the point where teachers, mentors, and friends pulled me aside very seriously to tell me that they thought I'd be famous someday. Now, that's a weird thing to be told as a kid, but of course I loved hearing it. Nobody knew exactly what they thought I would be famous *for*, of course; they just felt I had this unique ability to connect with people and make them laugh. And who doesn't love a good ego stroking at the age of six? They were right, too: I *really* wanted to be famous.

The thing is, I always hated being bored. When I get bored, I make stuff. At ten I wanted to have a mini-golf birthday, but the closest mini-golf place was over an hour away, and my parents said, "Why don't you just figure out a way to have it at home?" By the next day I had come up with a plan to build a nine-hole miniature golf course in the woods behind our house. I spent two weeks buying old putters and golf balls from thrift stores, gathering old bricks and rocks from the woods to make barriers and obstacles, and even getting some Astroturf from Home Depot to lay down on a few of the holes (I couldn't afford enough for all of them). I made a hole entirely from moss. I even had a hole that had the "ball goes in a hole and through a pipe to another part of the hole" thing. It was supercool.

Then my birthday came and it thunderstormed the whole day and the party was canceled. One of my first lessons was that making the product can be more fun than the product itself. Some people learn that with sand castles . . . I learned it with a nine-hole miniature golf course. I'm weird.

As I got older, I did stints as a juggler, unicyclist, parody musician, competitive Dance Dance Revolution player, award-winning French hornist, collegiate national champion improviser, touring performer, voice-over artist, and finally digital video producer.

In my early twenties, fame became much less of my goal. It was replaced with "I want to have fun and find the fun in everything I do." I also had a very firm belief in the philosophy of improv, which is "Yes, and." It's the idea that when someone presents information to you, you should accept it and then add to it. So in life, when someone wanted my help with something, I said, "Yes, and what else do you need help with?"

Pretty much every job I had led to my next job because of my positive attitude and my desire to learn everything I could while I was there. I made connections, gained skills, and then got an opportunity for something new! Somehow in four years I went

KEITH'S MOST EPIC FAIL

My most epic fail would probably be "The Try Guys Bake Bread Without a Recipe." I was excited to *finally* have the upper hand in a competitive Try Guys video. All these years of coming in third or fourth with Zach had finally paid off, and I, the chef of the group, would prevail. Except I didn't end up making good bread. None of us did, really. Probably because we didn't know what we were doing. Eugene, who was having the most fun, made the judge's "most tolerable" bread, and I felt totally defeated and upset that I didn't win. (See my face below for reference.) I was so miserable because I only cared about winning. But by only caring about winning, I really wasn't honoring the try to begin with. I wasn't having fun and appreciating baking. By caring so much about the victory, I had already lost. I wasn't entering into this try with the idea that I was going to learn and find an appreciation for baking. I wasn't using our own philosophy.

In my post-thoughts for the video, I was just angry. I totally lost sight of what mattered and what our audience could learn from our experience. The other guys were just like, "Keith you have to say something positive; we can't use any of this rant." But I couldn't get past it on the day of. Now when I look back I'm more embarrassed about my behavior than I am about my totally failed bread. Funnily enough, though, I still learned some things about baking from this shoot. I couldn't see past my anger to articulate them in the moment. But even though this was my biggest failure, I still learned how *not* to do an egg wash.

from performing in front of college students on a stage to performing in front of (mostly) college students on videos on their phones. I couldn't have planned out that journey in my five-year plan (do colleges still make you do those?). My point is that none of us set out to become The Try Guys. We all ended up here because we said yes to the sometimes random opportunities that led to this. And this isn't the endgame for us. It's just the most recent door we opened, and hopefully we'll never stop moving through them.

Now we are famous, I guess. And I'm proud that the four of us are famous for literally saying yes to so many opportunities. Sometimes people ask if it's annoying to get recognized. I tend to respond with "It's a great thing to have a lot of people like you. I'd be much more annoyed if I was famous because people hated me." I'm glad we can make people happy with our videos.

And I'm thrilled one of the doors I opened led me to Ned, Eugene, and Zach.

NED FULMER:
Renaissance Man

 I HAVE ALWAYS BEEN both an artist and a scientist. As a kid, I designed my own model rockets but also directed my own stop-motion movies. In high school, I was both president of the drama club as well as the AutoCAD designer for the robotics team. I was equal parts mathlete and comedian. After I graduated from Yale—

  Nobody cares that you went to Yale!

Guys, go away! This is my section.

Anyway, after Yale, I worked as an R&D chemist in a renewable fuels lab in Chicago for a good part of my twenties. But I soon found myself at an inflection point. It was steady work, if a bit boring at times, but to advance in my field of science stuff (that's the technical term), I would have to go to grad school for seven years to get a PhD, or more likely pivot to energy consulting and get an MBA. But as I was applying to a consulting job that would move me to the suburbs of Boston, a little voice told me I was making a mistake. Was I giving up my dreams?

You see, while I was doing science stuff by day, by night I was fulfilling my passion of performing comedy. I had been steadily working my way into theaters that I admired in Chicago. I performed on a weekly house improv team at the iO Theater. I had won some awards with my sketch group and put up shows at Second City. I had even auditioned for *Saturday Night Live* and done solo character acts.

And for all this glamour and success and laughs, damn it, I had gotten paid a grand total of twelve dollars and seventy cents. I used that to buy a burrito. *With guacamole.*

The thing is, the Chicago comedy and improv scene is absolutely incredible. I wouldn't trade those early years of doing midnight shows and getting onstage five, six, seven times a week for the world. I will absolutely treasure the training, the community, and the friends I made for life. But. Butttttttttt. It is very hard to make a living doing comedy there. There are a handful of top-tier jobs at Second City, some touring work, and the occasional commercial or TV show. In order to advance, most people move to either New York or Los Angeles. I had always wanted to be a TV writer and actor, so LA was my best bet. But I had neither a job nor any clue how to make that happen.

I was at a crossroads. Do I risk everything and move to LA, hoping it all works out? Or do I apply to grad school? Do I double down on my dreams, or accept the fact that not everyone makes it? Do I pursue scripts or spreadsheets?

I soon realized that I would always regret it if I didn't try taking a shot at LA. Grad school would still be there in two years (as would Los Angeles, now that I think about it, but I heard it's a young man's game). And between my network in the comedy scene in Chicago, and my network from, ahem, Yale, I figured I might be able to scrounge together a job in entertainment when I made it out west. Once I got to LA, one of those contacts, a very successful TV writer named Dave Goetsch, gave me the best advice I never knew I needed: *Forget TV*. Get involved in digital media instead. Make YouTube videos, make anything. TV will follow. But while you're young, don't spend your time getting coffee for people. *Spend your time making things.*

So I started a YouTube channel and made a bunch of parody music videos, celebrity impressions, and sketches with wacky characters I created. I filmed a whole bunch of stuff and, well, most of it was bad. But some of it was kinda okay! I submitted my kinda okay stuff along with an application for a BuzzFeed internship, and I got it!

At BuzzFeed, I found a really close community of collaborators doing like-minded things. And the best part about digital media? Spreadsheets! I had found a way to combine my two passions. You see, on the internet there is immediate feedback. Every click is a data point. And by studying which of my content got

NED'S MOST EPIC FAIL

My biggest failure in Try Guys history was the video "Ned Tries Famous Soccer Trick Shots," in which I tried to emulate trick shot legends and personal heroes Dude Perfect. But unlike Dude Perfect, who only shows the successes set to pump-up music, I wanted to show all of the failed attempts that led up to one successful shot. Now, I'm by no means a soccer superstar. Since breaking my leg in high school (much more on that in the next chapter), I've been playing much more defense, and much less offense. So, I wasn't sure if the video was even gonna work.

I was out on this soccer field by myself on a random Tuesday morning. It was hot. I was sweating. I spent the first hour pumping up thirty balls. Then I got to trying the trick shots. It was hard. Way harder than I'd imagined. I tried doing an "around-the-world" where you scoop your foot around the ball in the air. No dice. Next I tried to kick the ball into a basketball hoop. Not even close. Then I tried to hit a bowling pin from long range. Haha.

Finally, all I had left to try was a banana kick, aka the "Bend It Like Beckham," where you curve the ball around an obstacle and score a goal. I have always dreamed of lining up to take a free kick in a big game and curving a perfect ball around a wall of defenders and into the corner of the goal.

I tried this kick for hours. The balls soared over the goal, careened out of bounds. Everywhere but the net. I must have said to the camera, "Okay this is my final try," about twenty times. But eventually . . . I did it! On the sixty-seventh take.

You'd think this was a tale about perseverance, and to a certain extent it is.

But when I finally put the video online it completely flopped. It was one of our least-viewed videos of the season. It turns out that Dude Perfect is Dude Perfect for a reason. Nobody wanted to see all my misses. But as you'll learn in this book, embracing your misses is half the battle.

the most clicks, I found this amazing way to mix creativity with data. I was hooked. Plus, I met three other guys at BuzzFeed who would eventually become my best friends.

ZACH KORNFELD:
Basically Spielberg

 **I'VE WANTED TO TELL STORIES** my entire life. It all dates back to my early childhood depression (more on that later in the book; I bet you can't wait!). Or maybe it just stems from the fact that I needed some sort of after-school activity so I wasn't just sitting on my ass all day watching *Dragon Ball Z*. I dabbled in painting, music, and even took some comic book drawing classes. I started and stopped a dozen novels without ever getting past the first chapter (here's hoping I do better with this book). In middle school I wrote the world's worst movie screenplay—an ensemble comedy about a group of stock caricatures getting shipwrecked on an island that for some reason turns into a high-concept action movie . . . I don't really remember the fine details but the mafia was involved, something to do with smuggling drugs. But the real game changer came when I was ten years old and Lego released the Lego Studios Movie Maker Kit.

It was a full production kit, complete with sets, a camera, and rudimentary editing software, all endorsed by Steven Spielberg himself! It even came with a tiny Steven Spielberg Lego man that I still own and cherish to this day. The idea was to create stop-motion movies using your Legos, but after a few videos I realized I could broaden it to the rest of my bedroom, where, inevitably, I cast my stuffed animals in instant classics such as *The Bear Witch Project* and *Raiders of the Lost Bark*. I begged for a cheap camcorder for my next birthday, and from there I was off and running. Making movies became my passion, and that passion grew into an obsession.

While other kids were running around outside and chasing each other with sticks, I was sitting in my parents' basement learning iMovie and Photoshop. For those unaware, age thirteen is a big deal for Jews—it's bar mitzvah time, baby. I grew up in a town just north of New York City called Scarsdale, with a large and in-charge Jewish population, which meant for a year and a half I attended one to three bar mitzvahs every weekend. During just about every bar mitzvah, they make you sit down for these painfully slow and boring photomontages of the kid's life, set to the world's cheesiest music. Slow fades between photos with minor motion, some James Taylor playing in the background . . . a total snooze fest. I sat twitching in my seat during those first few bar mitzvahs and thought to myself, "I can do better." And so I did.

I quickly became the most in-demand bar mitzvah editor in all of Westchester County, thanks to my competitive rates and way above-average product. I'm not going to sit here and say I totally reinvented the genre, but I sure as shit added some pizzazz: revolutionary moves like actually cutting to the beat of the music and pacing the damn things up. Not gonna lie, though: the bar was pretty low.

And what's better, it meant that I never had to get a real job all throughout high school—I got to just keep practicing editing and having fun behind a computer. My passion became my job, and I was justified in spending all my time on it.

When I wasn't editing sappy montages and teddy bear opuses, I was working on that godawful screenplay. I was so proud of what I had written that I asked my parents if we knew anyone in Hollywood—this thing was gold, I thought, and surely if Paramount would just read it I'd be the hottest young writer on the scene.

Sure enough, my father's old buddy Rick was a working movie producer, and in the world's kindest gesture, he agreed to read a thirteen-year-old's 110-page script. Realistically, he got his poor assistant to read it, but hey, whatever it takes. Rick taught me two incredibly important lessons that still stick with me to this day. First, you get one favor from anyone in Hollywood, so choose wisely. He considered reading the script a freebie but the next time I needed something I'd better make sure it was good. And second: you're only as good as your life experiences. Rick's advice was less about the script and more about how you approach the world—wanting to be creative from a young age is fantastic, but you need to *live* to have stories to tell. I was spending so much time locked in a basement attempting to hone my craft that I had entirely neglected the most important ingredient of storytelling: cultivating knowledge and experiences to draw from. I've tried my best since then to really take that message to heart—to say yes to everything life throws my way, to remain open to new experiences, and to always explore the

ZACH'S MOST EPIC FAIL

This book is about how important it is to confront failure, but that doesn't mean it's always easy. Through prosthetics and makeup, we were transformed into bald men for "The Try Guys Go Bald." What was meant to be a fun exploration of a common male insecurity just so happened to be the absolute worst thing for my self-esteem. For years, I've tried to ignore that my hairline is receding. Anytime I see photos where it's clear my hair is thinning, a tiny bomb explodes inside my heart. It's the one physical trait about myself I truly, deeply despise, and facing it head on (zing) proved more emotionally draining than I'd expected.

A team of talented makeup artists came in, covered me in a bald cap, and blended the lines. Adding insult to injury, Ned and I were outfitted with the Friar Tuck look, a half-moon of hair tracing the back of our heads. Everywhere I went that day I was met with shocked gasps, laughs, and stares. It was . . . not a fun day. But in the long run, the experience has forced me to confront my relationship with my hair. It was a turning point in allowing me to accept that this is something that's really happening,

and ignoring the problem isn't about to make it just go away. I'm not going to tell you that you need to just accept everything about yourself; my hair is something that makes me feel bad, and so I've taken steps to do something about it. But I am going to tell you that addressing things is better than repressing them. I had to confront my nightmare in order to get out of it.

I came in with fears that bald Zach would look like a weird baby turtle instead of bald heartthrobs Dwayne Johnson, Bruce Willis, or Vin Diesel. I can confirm that I definitely don't look like any of those guys, but ultimately if I lose my hair, it's not going to be the end of me. I'll adjust, I'll adapt, maybe I'll become an underground street racer/international superhero (that's a Vin Diesel reference). Who knows, maybe by the time you read this I'll have already gotten fed up and just shaved it all off.

unknown. It's made me a better storyteller, and it's certainly made me a better person (I hope).

I carried that school of thought with me through college and when I entered a new job at BuzzFeed. There I was able to marry my absurd passion for creating with the advice of going out and living as much as possible. Oh, and another thing happened during those early days at BuzzFeed—I met the three ding-dongs with whom I'm writing this book.

EUGENE LEE YANG:
Black Sheep

FISH OUT OF WATER. Black sheep. Ugly duckling. Zoological idioms abound, but I will always be the friend who operates from a bizarre outsider's perspective. Although some may call my attitude somewhere between an unusual form of existential nihilism and darkly comic extreme self-awareness, I choose to label myself as defiantly un-labelable. My journey has been fraught with

Me

My sisters

My Mom

emotional pitfalls, deep physiological trauma, and cruel, constant reinvention—much of which you'll be reading about in later chapters.

In short, I am the last person anyone would have expected to end up as a digital viral star. The Try Guys were the last three characters I would have ever imagined becoming best friends with. Yet here we are.

I was born and raised in central Texas, where my parents, Korean immigrants, settled during the 1980s. My ancestors survived Japanese occupation and a civil war to relocate to, of all places, the conservative American South, where rampant racism was accepted as a daily norm. My childhood was informed entirely by feeling, looking, and lamenting my differences, and I was a charged, noxious bundle of extreme anxiety and self-loathing. I thought the world was a deadening, terrible hellhole from which there was no escape besides my myriad creative outlets, which included writing, drawing, theater, choir, dance, and music.

My family shares a rebellious streak. My parents divorced, which was rare for a religious East Asian family. Both of my sisters spoke their minds to the umpteenth degree, bucking any submissive stereotype. I, with no hope of becoming a lawyer, doctor, or engineer (the holy Asian trifecta), retreated into my own imagination. Filmmaking, as a wise middle school teacher would fatefully inform me, seemed to be a perfect career fit, and I set my sights on the University of Southern California's film school, where I was ultimately accepted.

Compounding my already tortured racial identity complex was the stark realization, early on in puberty, that I was queer, which for an ugly duckling who already was compromised by his looks was like getting the cruelest cherry atop a shit cake. I was stunted in ways I couldn't exercise healthily and did not feel comfortable in my own skin, sexually and ethnically.

So much of my self-perception was influenced by my otherness. I retreated further into artistic expression, unable to truly deal with my identity crisis until I was well into adulthood. My online work, especially with The Try Guys, actually helped my acceptance and self-esteem immensely.

After college, and after years of working in the industry as an edgy, furious music video and commercial director, I happened upon a job in digital video—both behind and in front of the camera—by total chance. It would turn out to be a monumental shift in my dreary, rebellious life.

There's a grand, almost depraved irony in how the international audience, billions over, were introduced to me: charming, self-assured, and "alternative," but palatably so. At BuzzFeed I stretched my acting capabilities and performed the more "relatable" side of my personality as part of our constant testing to reach wider audiences. Shockingly, it worked: viewers responded to my dryness (diluted apathy), sharp wit (controlled rage), coy inappropriateness (nonconformity lite), and brassy self-esteem (a willful need to be a strong minority figure). Many people found my point of view to be akin to theirs, especially when cast in direct contrast with the other Try Guys, and in a way I never dreamt possible I suddenly found myself representing people of color, the LGBT community, and those who felt "different." I, the bullied weirdo, was the internet's version of homecoming king. It was, and still is, utterly confounding to me.

I have become accustomed to this new path in life, working on my voice from the side of the light as opposed to the darkness. My apathy, rage, and nonconformist stances haven't thinned so much as they've evolved to express themselves in smarter, more effective ways. My work with The Try Guys—the unlikeliest of best friends—has consequently made me into a happier person.

Stars Are Born

In early 2014, the four of us joined BuzzFeed's fledgling video division in Los Angeles, which at that time was about a year and a half old and just starting to find its footing. There were under twenty video employees, mostly young, and all full of energy and zeal. We were hired first as interns, then full-time as junior producers with the goal of producing shareable viral videos. It was the early days of social content, and every day a group of passionate creators came in to test assumptions and try their hand at cracking viral formats. Some videos hit and others were phenomenal disasters, but every video was a new opportunity to learn.

We did everything back then, from manually adding captions to eating bizarre foods on camera. Every producer was responsible for six videos a month, start to finish, everything from conceiving the idea through execution, editing, and delivery. The speed all but assured that nothing we were making was perfect, but it also meant that we had an opportunity to try a million different things, learn constantly, and grow. The job was to understand what makes videos go viral, dissect the elements, test them, make more dope viral videos, rinse, and repeat.

When we started, we knew each other but we were on different teams, which were color-coded blue, yellow, red, and green. The blue team made videos for the yellow channel. These were confusing times. Keith was working on a small unscripted pod, Zach was on the comedy/scripted team, Eugene was making videos for the BuzzFeed Violet character universe, and Ned was training all the new hires while making science videos. We weren't friends and we seldom had opportunities to interact. Over the course of a few months, however, what was clear was that we were all talented video producers, and we were among the people we mutually found most fun to watch in videos. And, as we would soon find out, we were the only four willing to put *all* of ourselves on camera.

In September of 2014 we joined forces to produce our first video as a foursome. It was a video just like any other—another in a long series of tests—except this one required four subjects free of shame and willing to basically get naked in front of coworkers. We were both the producers as well as the only volunteers. "Guys Try On Ladies' Underwear For The First Time" was an instant hit (over 21 million views and counting, not that we're counting, but we are). Though the video itself was simple, we all had a blast, and we could all see the potential. That two-and-a-half-minute video would change the course of our lives forever.

Our story could have ended there. But then an unlikely bombshell hit. We woke up one fine November morning to the release of Kim Kardashian's *Paper* magazine cover. You know the one—she bared her naked buttocks to the world and "broke the internet," wearing nothing save for white gloves and a pearl necklace. Keith burst into the office full of energy and declared that we had to make a video about it, and we had to film it *today*.

We knew this was *a moment*—one of those rare, explosive internet events that everyone would be talking about. If we busted our asses (hehe), we'd be able to beat everyone and have the first video on it. We opted to stay late: just four guys, two bottles of champagne, and a whole lot of baby oil. When people ask when our bond really formed, we can easily point to that night. You get tipsy and oil up a coworker's butt, you become best friends real fast.

PAPER

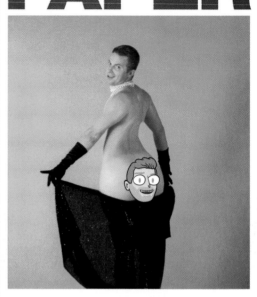

PAPER

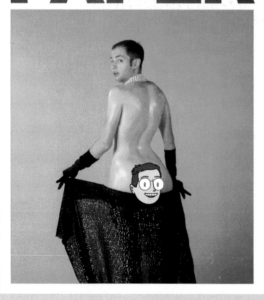

PAPER

PAPER

It took working eighteen hours straight to get it done, with all of us staying late to edit and Keith pulling a double shift. By noon the next day the video was ready to publish. We could feel it; this one was going to be big. Eugene said out loud to no one in particular that we needed a name, to which Keith replied, "I was thinking the same thing. Like, what if we call it 'Try Guys' or something." We debated the merits of "The Try Guys" vs "Try Guys" for longer than you'd think possible and landed on "The." (When in doubt, always choose the article.) The video exploded into one of the most-viewed videos BuzzFeed had ever released. *The Try Guys* were officially born.

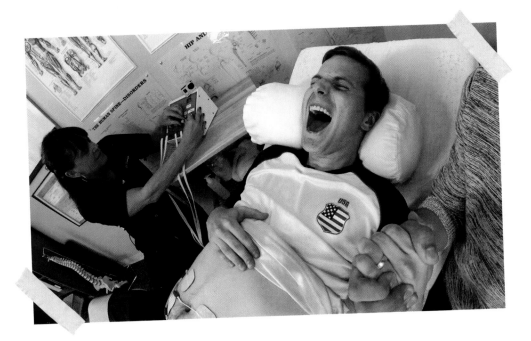

After that, we tried everything we could. We tried drag, we tried nude modeling, we tried hitting professional fastballs. We made a miniseries on K-pop and anime. We created a competition reality show for YouTube Red. We produced big-budget branded videos that took us across the country and went dog-sledding on a glacier in Alaska. We performed live shows at Vid-Con with security escorts and spoke at colleges to screaming

fans. We were trending worldwide on Facebook and had one video get more than 100 million views. We got recognized on the street, in Disneyland, even in foreign countries. Our videos were featured in an actual museum crediting us with pioneering the genre of "try" videos. We stopped making 2-minute videos and started making 20-minute episodes. We had somehow rapidly become internet famous and suddenly had . . . fans? A strange feeling for four producers with disparate interests. But we loved making videos together, and we were just getting started.

Throughout it all, we started to develop a philosophy. Try new things. Don't be afraid to fail. Learn from experts and be respectful. Experience all the beautiful, wonderful, and insane things this world has to offer. There were many people who helped us along the way, like our wonderful first producer Katie—secretly the fifth Try Guy—and, despite the bureaucracy and politics of a large corporation, together we fought to make content that we personally believed in. We worked to connect people through our videos, to make them smile, to help them learn, and to make the world a more open and accepting place.

Ultimately, though, we needed the autonomy of being fully independent to grow as creators. In April 2018, after four years and more than one hundred videos, the four of us put in our letters of resignation. We had tried surviving in the wildness, a demolition derby, cosplay, and *American Ninja Warrior,* but it was time to try the scariest, most difficult thing yet: starting a company of our own.

What's Wrong with You?

Now that you know enough about us to trust us with your life, let us help you roll up your sleeves. In order to change and improve and grow, you'll need to dismantle your bad habits. And in order to dismantle your bad habits, you need to understand *what* habits are and how they form in the first place. Thinking about this led us to the writing of Charles Duhigg, author of *The Power of Habit: Why We Do What We Do in Life and Business.* You have to read books to write books, baby!

According to Duhigg, we think we go around all day *choosing* how to live our lives, but 40 to 45 percent of what we think are decisions are actually just habits. There's a trigger, a behavior, and then a reward. And once a behavior turns into a habit, it becomes automatic and moves into the basal ganglia near the center of our skull. The basal ganglia is one of the oldest structures in our brain.

Yuck. How awful sounding is "basal ganglia"? Just knowing there's a ganglia deep in our basal controlling our caveman brains is haunting. But now you know; it's not your fault you can't resist a snack break at the same time every day, or that when you come home you watch two hours of TV instead of going to the gym . . . it's your basal ganglia. Fuck you, basal ganglia (seen below looking all creepy and shit)!

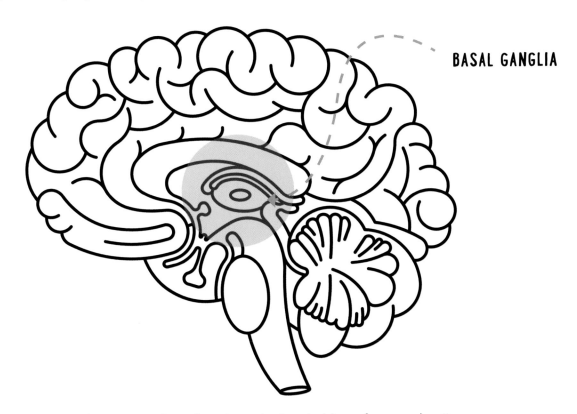

BASAL GANGLIA

Turns out there's something deep in our brain, a holdover from monkey times, that rewards and entrenches "comfortable" behaviors, making us slaves to our own habits under the guise of free will. And unfortunately, it's not so simple to change these habits. All of our triggers and routines and habits are jumbled up together. Getting a 3:30 p.m. cookie in the kitchen is as related to hunger as it is to stepping away from the computer. It took Duhigg a few days of observation to realize that what he actually craved every day was *socialization*, and so he was able to replace his daily cookie break with ten minutes of water-cooler chat. Less delicious, but a more direct satisfaction of his true desires (and easier on the hips).

So as you read this book, we want you to start thinking about some of the habits you've picked up, and how they've made you less vulnerable to new experiences. Do you eat at the same three places every day because you fear change? Do you avoid big parties because you get social anxiety/don't remember people's names/drink too much? Do you snooze the alarm forty-five times every morning? These are the things you want to break down and flush out of your system with some good old-fashioned failure. Duhigg might recommend a careful uncoupling of habits. Instead we're going to prescribe a shock to the system.

Success is stumbling from failure to failure with no loss of enthusiasm.

—*Winston fucking Churchill*

Get Ready to Try

People always ask us how we start a new try. It's simple. Take the thing you least want to do and jump right the fuck in.

We have an internal motto that the less we want to do something, the better a video it is. We'd extend that to say the less you want to do something, the more important it is for you to try. What's holding you back? What do you think is the worst thing that can happen? Let's challenge that. Don't just do something with the knowledge that you might fail—jump in and seek out your failure. We want you to confront the worst thing you think could ever happen, realize it's probably not so bad, and grow from it. We want you to get some things *wrong*. There's a reason we're called The Try Guys and not The Succeed Bros. First of all, we're not related. But more importantly, success should never be your goal; the goal is the experience.

Put another way, it's not about always hitting the mark; it's about creating new habits and shaking yourself from the patterns we all trap ourselves in. It's about living and it's about exploring and it's about not allowing anything—especially yourself—to hold you back. Whether it's bad habits or a lifetime of inertia or a fear of forging a new path, we all at some point face that paralyzing challenge of trying something new. We're here to help you break free.

When we're putting together a new try for a video, one thing we like to think about is: what do I want to get out of this? We've found that if we spend some time thinking about *why* we are about to do something we have no business doing, it makes jumping in just a little bit easier. For instance, sometimes in life we try stuff (say, snorkeling) because a friend invites us and we don't want to say no because her parents have a sick beach house. And other times we try stuff (say, magic) because we think it's cool and actually want to learn how to do it. (Disclaimer: Only two of the four Try Guys think magic is cool. Can you guess which ones? Tweet us! See, this book is *interactive*.) The more personal the reason, the more powerful your drive will ultimately become. Most of the things we'll talk about in this book are changes that accompany deeply intimate life goals. Thinking about the "why" is your first step to a successful try. Final rhyme of the book, we promise.

So let's do a little exercise. Close your eyes. Well, keep reading, but then close your eyes. Visualize the thing that you're the most afraid to try, the thing that you're most insecure about. It could be something physical or emotional. What would it mean to you to be able to conquer it? Why do you want to do it? Keep that in mind throughout this book, and at the end, you'll have the tools to go out and face that fear.

We also think you should set a goal that's just out of reach and work toward it.

If you want to try to start jogging (gross, we know) and you set your goal as only halfway around the block because you know you can actually accomplish that, you're also setting the bar really low for yourself. We say set the bar *too high* and then strive to reach it.

Finally, it helps to remember that everyone is going through the same things you are. WE ARE ALL FAKING IT. Everyone is terrified in their own way. Also: 99 percent of the time no one can tell that you're faking it or are terrified. We always think everyone is staring or laughing at us, but the truth is they're dealing with their own nonsense. Ain't nobody got time for you. In fact, it's pretty self-centered to think anybody has *got* time for you. Long story short: fake it till you make it and fail like no one is watching. Don't believe us? We're going to prove it.

Don't Fail Alone

We jump right into unfamiliar situations. Most of our videos are shot in one day and we get thrown right to the sharks. Literally. But we do it together.

You're not alone, and to prove that, we're going to fail along with you. Throughout this book, we're going to put our money where our mouth is and show you just how productive and transformative it is to confront failure. The four of us are each going to tackle long-ignored life goals, with a bonus shared goal to boot, and prove that anyone—*anyone*—can get better just by screwing up a little. We're turning our philosophy back on ourselves and confronting our biggest insecurities, and we're doing it for you . . . but we're also doing it for us.

While we will always be there with you in spirit, you should also tell your friends about what makes you uncomfortable and then try that thing together! It's much easier with the support of a team. Who are the three people that you could text right now and tell them your goals? Text them. We'll wait. It'll give us a quick pee break. Phew. Done? Much better. Holding one another accountable will be something we'll talk about a lot in this book. When you know you have a buddy by your side, trying and failing seems so much less daunting. Plus, there's always a photographer for the 'gram.

We sometimes consult experts to give us a little insight before each try. In this book we'll be talking to CEOs, vegan gurus, personal trainers, and interior designers, all in an effort to learn as much as possible from our failures. *Seek out those who are better at things than you are.* It sounds like it should be in a fortune cookie, but it's also important advice. And if you can't find an expert, read about what you're going to attempt. At the very least, google it. Knowing a bit more about what you have in store is very empowering. Don't do *too much* research, though, or you'll psych yourself out.

Together, we're going to go out of our way to screw up. Only then can the real growth begin. We fail all the time and you can, too! What's the worst that could happen? You get eaten by sharks? (Okay, maybe that's a bad example.)

Reward Failure

A lot of times people tell you to "accept failure," but we think you should "reward failure." Take the time to give yourself a pat on the back after you fail. Commend

A BRIEF HISTORY OF TRYING

Twelve different publishers rejected *Harry Potter and the Sorcerer's Stone*—TWELVE!—before someone gave J. K. Rowling a shot. Did she give up? No. And now she has a billion dollars and one of the bestselling books of all time, soon to be right behind this one.

yourself for putting yourself out there. (Treat yo self, as the kids say.) Ninety-nine percent of people in the world didn't try anything new today, so congratulations, you are officially part of the 1 percent. Make sure you have a good accountant to manage all that newfound wealth!

How do you reward failure? The same way you reward success! If you go out for pizza after you win the soccer game, you should go out for pizza when you lose the soccer game. Congratulate yourself on getting out there and competing and doing your best. We're not saying to ignore the failure and pretend like you won. You should talk and think about what your failures were and how you could do better next time. If you punish yourself for failing, though, you're more likely to give up. You are only associating negative feelings with your failure. Growth comes from trying, failing, and trying again. So failure is necessary! Reward it! Yay pizza!

> Our greatest glory is not in never failing,
> but in rising every time we fail.
>
> —*Con-fucking-fucius*

Try, Try Again

The rest of this book will divide up every single aspect of life into five neatly delineated chapters: Health, Style, Work, Love, and Family. We're gonna talk about important things like dating, fashion, and CrossFit. We're gonna do a deep dive into each of our backgrounds with select stories that showcase the rocky journeys that brought us here. It's gonna get *weird*. But it's also gonna get real. So there's one more thing we wanted to touch on before we really get started, and that's respecting the process and each other.

You're not gonna like everything you try in life, but someone else *will*. And different things are important to different people. So as The Try Guys we try (sorry) to keep an open mind and a positive attitude. You don't have to like what you're doing, but you should at least respect it. Some people wear corsets because they like them. Others wear them because they help with back problems. No two experiences are going to be the same, so take the time to learn about the people involved in the community just as much as the thing that you're doing. Try to understand people who are different from you. There's a story behind everyone and everything.

And most important of all: always laugh at yourself, never at others. Well, of course you can laugh at your friends. We will be laughing at each other a lot in this book. We just mean, don't be a dick, ya know? We're all on this blue marble hurtling through space together. Some of us have our shit together. Most of us don't. Life is stressful. Having a sense of humor helps. So please keep that in mind as you continue on this journey with us. We don't have all the answers. We're not always right. We're not perfect.

But we're trying.

CHAPTER TWO

Health

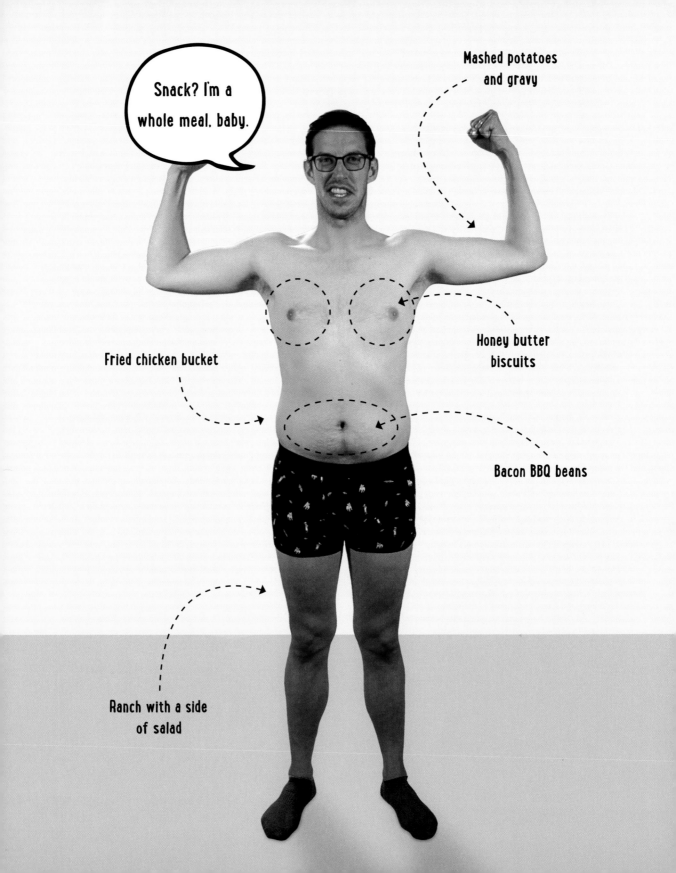

Although we may each resemble a chiseled Adonis, The Try Guys are not exactly the picture of perfect health. We have a cornucopia of physical and mental ailments that you are about to learn TMI about. And since the world is full of people and books telling you you're not hot enough or not fit enough or not *not* depressed enough, we want to jump on that gravy train, except steer it toward positivity.

Some of us love to work out: Eugene is a gym rat and Ned is an athlete. And some of us would rather stab our eyes out than pick up a dumbbell: Keith lacks the motivation to even try to get motivated and Zach's body hurts just thinking about it. But we do know that exercise is one of those habits that set off a chain reaction of positive goodness in one's life. Studies show that when people start exercising, they start using their credit cards less, procrastinating less, and even doing their dishes earlier. (Though let's be honest, anything is earlier than never.) So let's try—together—to develop some good exercise and eating habits.* But first let's take a trip down the memory lane of our not-so-fantastic athletic achievements. After all, in order to develop good habits, first you need to dismantle the bad ones. And we've got *a lot* of 'em. . . .

---

* All the health and exercise knowledge we are dropping is for informational purposes only. In fact, please make sure to consult a qualified professional before attempting anything in this book. (Yes, our lawyers made us say that.)

What's Wrong with Us

 BODY IMAGE is something I struggle with. I have a bit of a belly, my chest is a little more manboobish than I'd like, and I have zero upper-body strength. Because I'm tall and fairly filled out, the general assumption is that I'll have arm muscles like a normal human. But I don't. I really have none. If you get in there and give it a squeeze, you'll be reminded of those jelly-filled plastic tubes that were in the toy bins of science/discovery stores in malls. You try to squeeze it and it just flies out of your hands like a slippery fish-snake. My arms are weak little fish-snakes.

Some of this may come as a shock to people who watch me online, but I am really disappointed when I look at myself in the mirror before getting in the shower. I do a great job of spearing it with comedy all the time, but I do wish I was fitter like Eugene or Ned. It seems like such a daunting, life-changing task, and I'm afraid to make that leap.

In all honesty, this is something I've dealt with for a long time. Even as a kid, I remember being embarrassed that I was flabby when I was at my neighbor's pool. I would always sit up as tall as I could so my stomach would look less pudgy even when I was only eight or nine. But then at some point I decided I'd be a guy who eats. Partly this was to combat the idea that I needed to be skinny to fit in, and partly because I do really enjoy food. So I created the brand of a kid who eats everything. I would finish other kids' lunches, crush candy bars, eat snacks as soon as I got home from school. I even had the brief nickname of "human garbage disposal." Nowadays I still eat a lot, and I really like that I am an adventurous eater.

But I *also* have this fear of being unhealthy. I'm thirty-one, which isn't old, and I already find myself fatigued more than I think I should be. I can't jog more than a couple of blocks without needing to switch to a brisk walk. I've never done a pull-up in my life. And even when I do exercise, it's so few and far between that it makes no difference.

My wife, Becky—whom you will hear *a lot* about in this book—said something that really stuck with me. It was the idea that everything we do to not improve our health could one day take us away from our loved ones. That scares me the

A BRIEF HISTORY OF TRYING

Bethany Hamilton was a thirteen-year-old professional surfer when her left arm was bitten off by a fourteen-foot tiger shark. A month later she was back on her board and the next year she won a national surf competition. Think about that the next time you skip the gym because it's raining.

most, and should be my primary motivation for working out. But I'm embarrassed to go to a gym because I feel like I'm starting at such a worthless place, that I'm unfit (nailed it) to join in with people who have already dedicated their lives to this healthy journey. It's like being in the front row of an audience at a concert and the lead singer puts the mic to your mouth for the chorus but you don't know any lyrics and you just wore the shirt long enough for your cool friend to invite you OHGODOHGOD.

My personal mission throughout this book is to become a healthier person. I want to make over my diet and introduce consistent exercise into my daily routine. I want to be healthy enough to keep up with my kids and grandkids (someday). That's my "Why" and it's what is going to motivate me to do things I really, really don't want to do.

SO MUCH OF MY LIFE has been defined and shaped by my lack of physical ability, I don't even know where to begin. As shocking as it may be perusing through my childhood photos, I've always been horrible at sports. And in a suburb where your place in the elementary school social hierarchy was directly correlated to how many sports you played (and excelled at), that was a problem.

Most of my memories from childhood are of being winded and of desperately failing to run as fast as everyone else. Despite an early distaste for sports and the exceedingly obvious fact that I sucked at them, I was forced into athletic scenarios again and again and again (childhood really has a way of making you do the

things you hate repeatedly). Parents are left with two choices: let your kid wither away inside playing N64 (hell yeah!) or force them into after-school sports. My parents correctly and cruelly chose the latter. Baseball, basketball, tennis, swimming . . . I went through a rotation of after-school torture for years.

During Little League, I used to stand in the outfield and *literally* pray to God for fly balls to not come my way. Keep in mind I decided I was agnostic in first grade and had already dropped out of Hebrew school. (As a quick side note, if I ever become a rapper and/or rock star I'm going with *Hebrew School Dropout* as my debut album name. But I digress.) My communion with the Big Dude Upstairs would always go something like this: "Hey, God, it's Zach. Here's the deal—I know we don't talk much, but that also means I don't ask you for that much so maybe you could just do me this solid. If you get me through this game—fuck it, just through this inning—without a single ball coming my way, I'll take it as proof that you exist. I'll go back to Hebrew school. I'll even get baptized if that's your thing." And then a fly ball would come my way, I'd let it drop because of course I wasn't about to try to catch it, and two runners would score while my teammates recoiled in disgust.

Once a year, we'd be forced to take part in the Presidential Fitness Test, a government-mandated exercise regimen perfectly designed for public humiliation. We had to run three and a half laps around our big field, measured to equal one mile. Oh, the humanity. You ran around that field, careful to not step in geese poop, and every time you passed Go you were awarded a Popsicle stick. Three sticks in and you're done.

One year I decided I would beat the system. Right past Coach D'Angelo I spotted the box of spare Popsicle sticks. The heist was on. As I approached Coach D, I picked up the pace, showcasing my newfound athleticism. "Good running, Kornfeld!" he grunted in his short shorts. My con was working. I slowed to a stop, noticing my untied shoelace, and swiped a third stick from the box. I took the next lap nice and slow . . . I had to make my ending time believable. But when I handed in my three sticks, Coach D called me out on my bullshit. He was watching us closely and knew I had only passed him twice. Before I knew it I was back on the track, forced to run a third lap.

That third lap was one of the most humiliating (and exhausting) few minutes of my life as everyone else in my class waited for me to finish. Every time I slowed down, wheezing for breath, the kids at the finish line would yell for me to keep going. By the end I could barely jog. All this time I was unaware that there was one more person still running: Warren H. was in even worse shape than I was, with some medical issues to blame. But there he was, running behind me, and then next to me, giving it everything he had. The kids started cheering for Warren, chanting his name for him to push harder and beat me in what was now . . . a race? I ran with all the might my little body could muster and finished about two seconds before him. Then I collapsed in geese shit. I won the race, but what stuck was the feeling that I'd somehow missed the point altogether. You would think that whole experience would motivate me to work harder, but you would be wrong.

The first half of my childhood was defined by a cycle of profound sadness: I couldn't play sports, therefore I wasn't "cool," therefore I was worthless. I got depressed. And not "oh, no—Lady Gaga tickets are sold out" depressed. Like actually crying myself to sleep every night depressed. I had my midlife crisis in first grade. For those wondering, going to therapy as a kid consists of playing games designed to gauge your mental well-being. I remember playing the board game LIFE a lot (my therapist always seemed relieved that I wanted a family and a good job and to, you know, make it to the end of the game).

My depression lasted until I was able to discover things I *was* good at that

Try Guys Pups!

TRY GUYS HEALTH TIPS

* Morning yoga classes are the best if you force yourself to get out of bed. They're usually more low-key and all about stretching—what a lovely way to start the day (a yoga mat is basically just another bed)!

* You can't snack on junk food if you don't buy junk food .

* Your company is legally required to buy you a standing desk if you have a doctor's note. Alternate between standing and sitting every two hours to avoid turning into a human question mark by age forty.

* Go on a ten-minute walk after lunch. It's a great midday reset, clears your mind, and helps you digest that pizza you swore you wouldn't eat for a third time this week.

* Get a dog that's more fit than you. Or just borrow someone else's.

BOWIE
(ZACH)

EMMA AND PESTO
(EUGENE)

BEAN
(NED)

other kids didn't talk about, like art and storytelling and writing comics and creating weird worlds inside my head and making people laugh. I remember sitting in class one day and learning about famous filmmakers and artists who struggled with depression. There before me was a list of some of the greatest thinkers, artists, and writers the world had ever seen, and they were messed up just like me! It was a tremendously impactful moment in my young life that made me feel okay to be different. Now, I wasn't unathletic; I was an *artist*. And artists are allowed to sit in the shade during recess. It was the ladder I needed to help lift me from depression, but it also served as an anchor for me to totally neglect my physical health for years to come.

MY PERSPECTIVE on diet and fitness has always veered toward the extremes. Being fit and the picture of perfect health wasn't an option for me growing up: it was a requirement. In fact, it's the first thing my parents still ask me about when they call me to check in: "Have you been exercising? What are you eating?" Workouts and meals are the first things my sisters schedule when we visit each other. The idea that others had the choice to eat like shit or never lift a weight is beyond comprehension to me. I was taught to believe that one's physical dexterity leads to superiority in all other aspects of life. Keith and Zach have discussed their lack of motivation. My dilemma has always been the self-control to stop sprinting at breakneck speed.

Where does this intense need to "be well" in my family come from? As Korean War survivors, I imagine that survival was always near the top of the list for my grandparents and parents, and to be unable to move quicker or eat better than others led to a less fortunate station in life. East Asians, in particular, do whatever is in their power to get ahead. This was even more pressing for the immigrant generation as they moved to another country, desperate to provide for their children, but also to prove that they could progress beyond the ruling class's perception of them. To condition oneself and one's kids to be smarter, run faster, and look prettier than others only furthers their chances of making something big out of the little that Mom and Dad had to carry on their backs from the old country.

My sisters and I were born and raised in small-town Texas. Though we weren't running away from mortar shells or invading armies, we were taught that if we fell short of physical perfection, we were somehow "less than." And to maintain one's elite form, we would do anything in our power to rise above the rest of the pack.

I played, or at least tried to play, nearly every sport growing up. But when I focused more on the arts in high school, I suddenly gained weight. I vowed to change immediately. I ran five miles every morning and stopped eating for an entire summer, and in three months dropped almost forty pounds. Many might say that it was a particular form of anorexia that I briefly suffered from, but I claim very little emotional trauma (that I can remember) from that event. It was merely a means to an end. The grand irony is that in the pursuit of peak form I took extremely unhealthy measures to attain a certain goal in my mind.

The pressure from my family to stay fit has been a double-edged sword. I think it's conditioned me to have an unhealthy attitude toward my body image, but it has also made me appreciative of the hard-ass approach to getting stuff done.

A bruise is a lesson . . . and each lesson makes us better.

—*George R.-fucking-R. Martin*

FOR ME, health has always centered on strength. It's not about looking good. It's about feeling strong. I hate the feeling of weakness that is associated with being injured. Unfortunately, I've always been one to get injured a lot. I want to be able to actively play with my children (and easily get up from chairs) when I'm older. The fear of not being able to move around fully in the future is what drives me to be healthy today.

Like the other Try Guys, growing up I too was exposed to the hierarchy of cool imposed by athletic prowess. Being a generally athletic guy, you'd think that

WORKOUT BUDDIES

I've never had a "workout buddy." Right now Becky and I are kind of workout buddies, but we don't really like the same workouts or time schedules. Maybe I've never had workout buddies because *I* am not a workout buddy. It takes two people to like something and each other to be buddies about it.

is where the story would end—with me drowning in coolness. But alas, no. At all levels of fitness, it is always possible to feel like you still need to achieve more. Any experience in which I was picked last left me feeling mediocre and has driven me to be that much better.

I remember one awful story from the elementary school playground when I was picked to play goalie in a pickup soccer game. My team started off with the ball and everything was going well. They were passing it back and forth. I was alert, looking for a potential breakaway from the other team, ready to spring into action at a moment's notice. Then something curious happened. There was a turnover. But instead of dribbling the ball toward me, the other team turned around and tried to shoot on their own goalie.

It had turned into a *half-court soccer game*. I didn't even know that was possible. I was about fifty feet away from the game, so all my shouting was falling on deaf ears. I was extremely hurt and embarrassed. It's one thing to be picked last, but it's another thing entirely to be tricked into not even playing at all. At my favorite sport, no less. It's a very painful memory for me. But rather than closing me off from sports, it drove me to try that much harder.

THERE WERE TIMES I dabbled in working out. It was always some friend who convinced me it would be fun to hit the gym together. And, honestly, it is *way* more fun to exercise with a friend. You get to joke around and gossip instead of being forced to just listen to the sound of your own heavy breathing.

You hold each other accountable, you push each other, you keep each other in check. But, eventually, your schedules don't match up, and one missed appointment becomes seven, and before you know it you're only paying the gym membership to give yourself mental satisfaction that you *could* go to the gym. A true workout buddy partnership requires commitment on both ends.

I LOVE TEAM SPORTS way more than going to the gym, because the sense of camaraderie from being on a team is energizing. If you don't show up to soccer training or a game—you're letting your team down. It's like that with workout buddies.

I'VE TRIED doing fitness videos with Becky twice, and both times we bailed partway through as the challenge became too tough. We might benefit from a third-party workout buddy, because both of us are too good at appealing to each other's emotions and letting each other off the hook for breaking the diet or not exercising. We dieted for the wedding, and that gave us a real goal. We both gave up beer (and tried to drink skinny cocktails) and ate generally healthier. Without a big goal like a wedding, we find the motivation tough. And methinks drinking five skinny cocktails in a sitting doesn't quite have the effect I want it to.

Too Scared to Try

BY THE TIME high school rolled around, I settled into myself. Well, not really . . . new insecurities, new facades . . . but let's call it Zach 2.0 (still in beta but ready to roll out to a test audience). I was forming my sense of self, and that sense apparently had no concern for his body. I ate like shit. Fun fact: I didn't eat a single salad until I was twenty-two.

 Fuck salads.

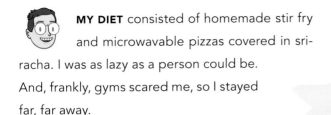 **MY DIET** consisted of homemade stir fry and microwavable pizzas covered in sriracha. I was as lazy as a person could be. And, frankly, gyms scared me, so I stayed far, far away.

Over the years I've found myself in a place where I'm suddenly down on myself again and catch that urge to get into shape. I see my reflection in the mirror and marvel at how impossibly scrawny I am; or I realize I haven't had a vegetable in a month. The weight of wanting to change is heavy, and instead of it fueling dramatic life reform, it usually ends up serving as fodder for self-loathing and doubling down on counterproductive behaviors. I cover up the bad feelings with even worse habits.

MY FEAR of the gym comes from when I moved from Tennessee to Illinois to finish my last year of high school. In Tennessee, the physical education requirement was only one semester. There wasn't much structure, just a football or basketball coach who would be like, "We're doing this game/activity today, or you can walk around the gym the whole class." But Illinois? Oh shit. You have to take gym *every semester of high school*. You could do badminton, volleyball, handball, basketball, floor hockey, swimming, running, etc. Because it was a new start at a new school, and I was in the familiar "skinny fat" body type that I've always had, I decided I'd make a difference in my life and take the weight-lifting class.

HOW TO FIND A WORKOUT BUDDY

Find a friend who loves to exercise and join them on a run or something they already love! Be up front that you're kinda nervous that you aren't as fit as they are, and that you'd love to get better. Flatter them! Tell them you admire their commitment. (Lie if you have to.)

Find someone who, like you, doesn't exercise but wants to try. See if you can convince them to go on a walk or run with you. Maybe just take a Frisbee to a park. Not all exercise needs to be running or lifting weights. Anything that gets you moving is awesome.

Find a place that you want to exercise and, even if you're scared, go in and ask how to try it out. Take a class, and after it's over talk to some of the people there. If you start with a compliment and follow up with a question about how to do something, they'll totally give you advice and be thrilled to talk about something they are good at. If it's a class, it's likely going to have the same people every week. You'll see familiar faces, and eventually you'll find some buddies there.

Much to my dismay, I realized on the first day that the only people who took weight lifting were the football players. I, a weak new kid, was in a room with giant men trying to out-masculine one another and push themselves to extreme limits. People were dicks to each other constantly, and I just tried to keep to the other side of the room, sitting on machines I didn't know how to use and avoiding any conversation. I'm normally a chatty guy, but this put me in such a gross environment for half a semester, so I ended up transferring out and into the badminton class, *which fucking ruled* but also wasn't the most helpful to my physique.

There's only one time I ever *really* sought out something that made me exercise, and that was Dance Dance Revolution. It had the same effect on the nerd community as Pokémon Go. People who played this game actually got into great shape. And since it was about one dollar per five to eight minutes of game play, it ended up being a pretty cheap gym membership, if you lived close enough to an arcade. I was so into DDR. I played for hours at a time for about a year of my life, and I was probably at my fittest (but still no upper-body strength, because DDR was all cardio). I would love to find something like that again, or maybe I should just buy a DDR machine for fifteen thousand dollars and play it every day while holding weights. I think I'd still commit pretty hard to DDR if I had the chance. I'm embarrassingly good at it.

 I NEVER SUGARCOAT. Instead of pushing friends as hard as I push myself, I pull them up toward me. It's a tactic I plan to do with Keith and one I've dreamt of since I've met him—to see him actually, willingly enter a gym and work out excites the teacher inside me. He needs to try CrossFit.

 Yes! Amazing idea. CrossFit!

What? Ugh, fine.

Keith Tries CrossFit!

ALL RIGHT, so even though I am terrified about going to a new gym where I don't know the movements and everyone is in better shape than me, I'm sucking it up and trying an intro class at Ned's CrossFit gym. Zach is coming along with me (workout buddies!) and we are learning the basics before all four Try Guys work out together later in the week.

We meet the owner/instructor JP, who is nice, considerate, and very encouraging. He tells us he'll push us appropriately while also driving us to a goal with proper technique. I feel just slightly less nervous.

We start by doing a WOD thing (workout of the day) that is meant to test our current level of fitness. We are supposed to row 500 meters, do 40 air squats, 30 sit-ups, 20 push-ups, and 10 pullups (ring pulls for our little bodies), all in nine minutes. I strap my feet into the rower, and look to Zach who has a similar look of dread on his face. Pulling the handles to my chest, I think, "This is easy, no problem!" but within a minute I am feeling fatigue set in. JP encourages us to finish the 500 meters and move on to the air squats. It's a nightmare. With each squat, my thighs burn and my speed peters out. I'm in unbelievable pain by squat 20, and am realizing just how out of shape I am.

Zach is similarly distraught, but he finishes his squats ahead of me and drops to the ground for the push-ups. I follow suit, soon to discover that my arms match my thighs in their unpreparedness. I feel like giving up almost immediately after beginning the push-ups. It's embarrassing to not be able to do more than ten at my age, but JP is pushing us and keeping things positive, somehow motivating us to keep going. He's also been correcting our form every step of the way, emphasizing safety above all. Zach and I start to do our sit-ups, but the time runs out (thank God!) as we collapse to the floor, faces red and jaws agape. I've never been so exhausted, which probably means I've never really pushed myself to the limit I need to in order to get results. Also, you don't know that you're doing things wrong until you have someone to help you do it right. JP made that last lesson easy.

EXPERT ADVICE FROM JP AMISTOSO

JP is the owner and head coach of CrossFit Ganbatte in Los Angeles. He's one of the top CrossFit coaches in the country and has also completed twenty-five marathons and ten Ironmans. No biggie.

Here are his tips for trying CrossFit for the first time:

* Come in with a mind-set of learning and *no ego*.

* Focus on your form and don't hesitate to ask questions. Your coaches will be more than willing to help.

* Every single movement is scalable to your strength and experience level so you can build as quickly or as slowly as you need.

* Eat something light ninety minutes before class and drink lots of water.

* Remember to cheer on your fellow athletes!

After ten minutes pass, I'm still very tired and alarmingly sore, but . . . I also feel good? Somehow, I'm looking forward to the next class with all the guys.

• • • •

A week has passed since the intro class, so my soreness has finally started to go away. Today we're trying CrossFit in a normal class with other people—not just me and Zach. We learn the push press (pushing the barbell from shoulder level to over my head). I have a few CrossFit friends, and they are always lifting big barbells overhead in their Instagram stories. I have never been able to see myself doing that. When JP said that was what we were about to do, I was very nervous. It just seemed like something that you could easily hurt yourself doing.

But I did it! As it turns out, JP didn't want me to hurt myself either, so everything is really scalable. I learned the muscle movements with a lightweight piece of PVC pipe, then a 15-pound bar, then upped it to 35 pounds, then 50, then 55, then 65. Sixty-five pounds is not a huge amount for a real weightlifter, but for me it was just the right amount to be challenging while maintaining safety. And I'm

BEFORE THE REAL CROSSFIT CLASS

STRENGTH:
10min EOMOM: (Every 2 Minutes)
2 Push Jerk @ 75%
WOD:
4RFT: (12min cap)
50' Weighted Walking Lunge
15 GHD Sit-Up

genuinely excited to try it again and slowly ramp up the weight!

While CrossFit can be intimidating from the outside, it's actually a really great place for beginners to learn form and technique. From the two classes I've taken, I now know how to do eight exercises safely. I know what weights I can handle. I know that my weakness is endurance. If I did this for a few more weeks and decided I didn't love it, I'd still come away with a bounty of knowledge that I could take into future workouts.

Am I fully over my mental blockage of working out? No. There were still plenty of times in the class where I felt inferior and intimidated by the strength of the other athletes. It's not something that's going to change over a couple of classes. There's always going to be something you're insecure about that's going to mentally try to drag you down, but having friends and trying something (even though you think it will suck) is a really good way to battle that little voice in your head. So, next time your friend invites you to a workout, or a health food place, why not say yes?

Fast-forward. It's now the next day and I'm very, very, very sore. What did I think would happen? Why does my butt hurt so much? Where are my legs?

Zach's License to Ill

 I'VE BEEN PLAGUED by nagging back pain on and off my entire life—how many kids do you

know who complained of a bad back in elementary school? I'm literally so Jewish it hurts. Back then, we thought the culprit might be those eighty-pound textbooks kids are forced to lug around. A brief flirtation with backpack alternatives didn't fix me, but it did prove to me that kids will *always* kick a wheelie backpack when it passes them in the hall. In high school, I developed debilitating hip pain, which would regularly eradicate my ability to sleep. I would wake up at night with excruciating pain shooting through my hips, unable to move or fall back asleep. A few months of physical therapy were enough to knock the symptoms into submission and gave me all the permission I needed to never think about it again.

Over the next few years, symptoms slowly crept out of the woodwork—fast enough to fill my days with pain, but slow enough that I was able to write it off as normal. I still had back pain, but everyone has back pain, right? I worked at a desk all day, my posture wasn't great . . . checks out. But there would be times when I would cough and a deep, sharp pain would radiate from my back through to my rib cage. Or my hips would stiffen up again, or an inexplicable discomfort would nestle itself deep within my spine. Throughout this process, I'd ask my doctor or my chiropractor if something more was wrong with me, but both wrote it off. Without visible symptoms, they had no reason to take my pain seriously, and I in turn was left doubting my own account of how I felt. Before I knew it, I was living with a baseline of pain every day to the point where I'd forgotten what it was like to not hurt anymore. It was all I knew.

Acknowledging my pain meant acknowledging I had to change, and I wish I could say I got there on my own. Really, it took things getting as bad as possible, progressing to a point where I couldn't sleep, I couldn't concentrate, and I could hardly stand to live. I really felt like a shell of the person I once was, and it had started affecting me in every aspect of life. Even then, it took the insistence of my girlfriend before I was ready to return to my doctor and finally advocate for myself, refusing to leave his office until he came up with a plan and a referral. I still remember going back to my doctor—the one who had confidently told me nothing was wrong year after year—and screaming, "I'm losing my fucking mind, don't tell me nothing is wrong, just fucking do something!" Part of me cringes at that memory,

knowing Margo Kornfeld raised her son better than that. But the other part of me beams with a quiet pride, grateful that I was finally strong enough to fight for my own well-being, even if for just a moment.

In the summer of 2017, I was diagnosed with ankylosing spondylitis (or AS, for short), an autoimmune disease in which bone grows where there shouldn't be. I know that makes it sound like I'm one of the X-Men but I promise it's not anywhere close to that cool. In broad strokes, AS is a disease that causes fusion in the bones, fills your body with inflammation, and makes you stiffen up when you're immobile, such as sitting at a desk or sleeping. In even broader strokes, my body hurts, and it hurts more when I'm not active. And I'm not active, like, a lot. I know people assume we're out shooting videos all the time but I'd say 80 percent of my life is spent hunched over a computer, lounging on a couch, or sleeping. At the time of my diagnosis, my hips had already begun to fuse, there were some bone spurs growing off my spine, and I had a pretty high level of inflammation throughout my body. After conquering the difficult task of learning how to pronounce it (kind of like the dinosaur ankylosaurus, if that helps), I next had to learn how to live with it.

Getting a diagnosis and a prescription for medication should have been the beginning of an effortless cruise into feeling amazing, but if this process has taught me anything, it's that treatment is a bumpy road.

The sad truth is, I stopped paying attention to my disease the first moment I started to feel better. Instead of keeping up with my recommended physical activity and diet—things intended to promote my long-term ability to combat the disease and hopefully one day enter remission—I took the newfound relief from my medicine as permission to entirely ignore my responsibilities. I stopped researching AS, I severely slacked on exercising, and I tried my best to stop thinking about it altogether. I didn't want to know more about disease, because the more I learned about it, the more real it would become.

Within six months, the effects of my medicine started wearing off as my body developed antibodies. The fact that I'd slipped back into poor habits also meant that my body was even less equipped for everything to come. What's followed has been almost a year of testing new treatments, trying to find the medicine

and life habits that are right for me. It's been a pretty frustrating and repetitive cycle, and if nothing else, it's proven to me that you can't wait until things are at their worst to start prioritizing self-care and exercise in your life. It's a lesson I wish I could've learned without having to experience it firsthand, but unfortunately for me, I've needed to relapse again and again before I could finally listen to the obvious.

There's no force in this world more powerful than inertia, except maybe Thanos once he's collected all the Infinity Stones (we still making *Avengers* jokes in whatever year you're reading this?). The only thing harder than willing yourself to get up off the couch is manifesting a fundamental upheaval of life habits, and that's true even when you know it's imperative to your overall health and happiness. No part of this is easy—I've been struggling with it for nearly thirty years and still do. But on the flip side, we can bring in another science metaphor and point out that objects in motion stay in motion. Once you get new habits in place and develop patterns toward a healthier, happier life, it's much easier to maintain. I look back at something as simple as building in thirty extra minutes to walk my dog every morning—once a Herculean undertaking to work into my busy life, and now something I genuinely look forward to as part of my wake-up routine.

When I'm cursing at my alarm clock, moaning that it's too early to get out of bed, let alone exercise, I find that it's helpful to have a "why"—a reason

GETTING OFF THE COUCH

Try the exercise that scares you the most. Whether it's CrossFit, roller derby, or just going to the gym itself. Don't be afraid that it will be too hard—*know* that it will be too hard. Like, be safe and let the instructor know that you're new, but be okay with having moments in the class that are too challenging. Find out if it is really as scary as you thought. Maybe you'll leave hating it or maybe you'll leave loving it, but at least you won't fear it anymore. You tried it. Now try it again or try something else. Just keep moving that needle toward your goal.

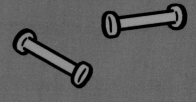

for the goals you've laid out. A why can totally clear the path when you're in your own way. My biggest fear isn't how my disease affects my physical well-being, but rather how it relates to my relationship with my girlfriend, Maggie (don't worry, much more on her later in the book). Already it touches us in ways I wish it wouldn't. There are times I just need to lie down instead of being up and active. On bad days, there are household chores I can't help with (the best get-out-of-heavy-lifting card nature ever invented). But really, I think about our future. I don't want her to have to care for me. I don't want her to have to worry about me, or pity me, or slow down her life so I can keep up. And most of all, I fear not being well enough for the children I hope for us to have someday. It's clear to me that I need to get my shit together if I want us to have a happy future together. With that in my mind, I have the fuel I need to finally get over the hump that's been holding me back.

Earlier this year I made it my job to care for myself. To prioritize exercise in my schedule and monitor how I feel every day. Stretching twice a day, exercise throughout the week, long walks with my dog every morning, monitoring the food I eat, avoiding activities I know cause flare-ups, experimenting with alternative treatments, listening to my body and finally hearing what it has to say!

And after all that . . . I feel okay. I still have a baseline of pain most days. My neck is pretty stiff even as I'm typing this out, and my hips are pretty sore, which reminds me I should switch to standing while I write. I'm far from perfect when it comes to sticking to my routines. I have flare-ups. I've had complications with my medicines. Some nights I still just don't sleep. I said it before and I'll say it again—treatment is a bumpy road. In truth, changing all at once can be totally overwhelming and cause you to just shut away from the world. So, baby steps, introducing one habit at a time, and we'll get there.

As the poet and philosopher Drake once observed, "You only live once." I think he meant that to say, "Fuck it, another round of tequila shots for the table," but I prefer the idea that you can only feel as good as you allow yourself. You get one life, one body, one go at this whole thing. Make yourself your own responsibility and let's get living.

I can accept failure, everyone fails at something.

But I can't accept not trying.

—Michael fucking Jordan

No Pain, No Gain

WHEN I DON'T EXERCISE or if I have a spell of eating bad foods, I spiritually feel like utter shit. There's no other way to describe it—my entire being becomes bogged down by this idea that I'm physically worthless. My sisters and I will toss around the word "ugly" as the catch-all term for when we don't feel our best. "I'm ugly." "I'm ugly." "I'm ugly." We say this, I think, to always remind ourselves that we have to work hard to keep up any goodwill we've built from our countless workouts and salads.

That attitude to "man up" and work through the pain has manifested itself in various ways in how I treat my body. I rarely take medicine when I'm sick. I've never rested an injury. The idea that I can triumph through sheer will, regardless of how much I hurt, has trumped any logic when it comes to how detrimental such an outlook is to my overall health.

But let's talk about the positives this outlook brings to the table, especially among my group of friends. I am a grand motivator when it comes to committing to an exercise or diet regimen. Although my internal dialogue is harsh, my external communication is supportive and informative. It's a more life-affirming way to channel the wealth of discipline and impossible goals I've constructed in my mind. My older sister, who is, for lack of a better term, a hard-core self-proclaimed bitch, taught Pilates for years after she'd get off work at her law firm. Why? Because she liked motivating others, just like me.

For example, it's not always captured in a final edit, but in every Try Guys video where a physical challenge is presented, unless I was absorbed with going head-to-head with Ned, I tried to help the others make it through challenges that were far more demanding on their bodies than mine. I've personally choreographed and staged all of our live performances, and a week of intense rehearsal leading up to a twenty-minute-long VidCon show really takes a toll on Keith and Zach especially. As the instructor I have to positively reinforce my students in order for them to shine. There's nothing more rewarding than watching my friends succeed in areas where they're more scared than me. It's the best kind of medicine and a sign of my gradual evolution: accepting that I'm not "ugly" or a punching bag for pain, but in fact someone whom others look toward as a leader who inspires confidence.

– – – VidCon rehearsal

Ned's Achilles' Heel (Well, Knee)

 IN HIGH SCHOOL, I broke my leg playing soccer and it changed my life. On this particular play, I received a through-ball from the midfield and started running past the defenders. I was faster than the defense. But the ball was still just out of my reach. I was sprinting as fast as I could, trying to catch up to the rolling ball. The keeper started to run out. To me as a fourteen-year-old, scoring a goal was the only thing that mattered. I ran as hard as I could and reached out to flick the ball away from the goalie. And suddenly, *crunch*. We reached the ball at the exact same time. I tapped it. But he smashed it. The goalie, sliding, hit me with his whole body in a powerful position. My foot got planted underneath the ball, awkwardly.

We both recoiled. I screamed out. I was shattered. I immediately knew something was horribly wrong with my leg. I ripped off my sock: my shin was bent. My leg suddenly was curving in a way it was not supposed to. It was gross. Fortunately, nothing broke the skin, so there was no blood. It immediately started swelling and I lay back down, nearly blacking out from the pain.

The rest of the day was a blur of ambulances, doctors, and morphine.

I was in a cast up to my hip all summer, and it would be fifteen months until I could play contact sports again.

It was this injury that led me to develop an interest in theater and film. Previously, I only liked sports and cool science stuff. But when I broke my leg, I watched movies and read plays all summer. I developed a love for comedy.

The school year started and since I was still in a walking boot, I chose to do theater after school. My first part ever was a largely nonspeaking role called Cue Card Guy, who got disemboweled by a harpy before the play was halfway over (it killed). It was an iconic original work, written by a fellow student. Immediate Tony consideration. In any case, I was hooked.

Another big injury that changed my life and brought me inevitably closer to The Try Guys happened mere months after my wedding. In October 2012, I split my knee open down to the bone playing paintball in rural New Hampshire. There were paintballs flying by me and I tried to slide down on one knee for cover. It turns out, when you run full speed through a wooded course, sliding on your knee is not the best idea. My knee smacked a rock. Direct hit. It was a familiar feeling, nearly the same

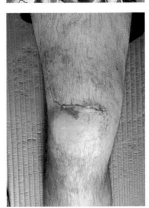

as breaking my leg ten years earlier. My college friends who were with me that day describe it as "The Day We Saw Ned's Kneecap for the First Time." Actually, that sounds like a good parody for a BuzzFeed video.

I had a partial tear in my quad tendon but the real damage came when, after a surgery to clean everything up and sew up the tendon, my knee joint got infected. Since we were playing in converted farmland, there was all sorts of soil bacteria that, once it gets inside the skin, can be dangerous. My whole body was shaking. I had fevers and chills. They gave me a clicker to dispense morphine and I remember clicking it over and over. They transferred me from rural New Hampshire to Massachusetts General Hospital, in downtown Boston. My wife, Ariel—whom you will meet at length later in the book—and my family flew out to be with me. I had two more surgeries to open everything up and clean it out, while being given the most powerful antibiotics they had. I was told half-jokingly that if it were the 1970s, I would have lost my leg or even died. I don't remember much from that time. Just flashes here and there. Ariel lying next to me on the room's couch. My sister placing a cool washcloth on my head. My mom bringing in bagels. My dad rolling me in a wheelchair.

I ended up staying in the hospital for three weeks. By the end, my leg had lost so much muscle and my knee had stiffened up so much that I could only bend it a few degrees back and forth. Once officially discharged, I began the process of recovery at my grandparents' house in Boston. I still had to take IV antibiotics, so every day Ariel would help me inject a syringe of yellow liquid into a tube that was continually attached to my arm. My only real duties throughout the day were to

A BRIEF HISTORY OF TRYING

Dick Fosbury failed to even qualify for track meets as a sophomore in high school, so he invented a whole new technique for the high jump called the Fosbury Flop and revolutionized the sport 4EVA. What have you done lately?

work on extending the range of motion in my leg. A few times a day I would strap my leg into a contraption that would ever so gently flex my joint back and forth until 2–3 degrees could turn into 5 or 10 or 20.

I was in so much pain that I couldn't function, I couldn't sleep. And this was when I developed a reliance on painkillers.

The few times a day that I took the drugs were the only times that I was pain-free. Of course, in the beginning, I really needed them. But eventually I was well enough to get my IV line removed and fly back to Chicago. I started physical therapy three times a week with my new friend and confidant, physical therapist Terrance. However, I continued to take the painkillers.

My 20-degree range of motion increased to 40 and then to 90. I could walk unassisted. At the time, I was on disability leave from work. I had nothing to do during the day but physical therapy. I felt the pressure to be creative, to write scripts, but my brain was constantly foggy. I ended up just watching all of *Breaking Bad* and playing *Halo: Reach* with strangers online. They all thought it sounded awesome to not have to work all day and watch TV. But without a purpose, it was hell for me. At least in high school, I had the impending deadline of going back to school. At this point in my life, I was a comedian doing improv and sketch at night and an R&D scientist for a renewable energy lab during the day. I couldn't do either of those things. Ariel was very supportive, yet I dreaded telling her the truth. At the end of a long day, she would casually ask, "What have you been up to today?" and what was I supposed to say? "I took prescription narcotics several times and tried to bend my leg a little while lying on the couch for eight hours straight." It was embarrassing to face the facts.

In retrospect, it was a really scary time. I can totally see how many stories of opioid addiction start with that same slippery slope. I know fully well that my story pales in comparison to other stories of addiction, but, even so, it was hard to stop taking those pills. I was so depressed at the time that they were one of the few things I looked forward to.

It was through conversations with Ariel and Terrance—the two people I saw pretty much every day—that I was finally able to stop. I remember a day where

I mentioned hydrocodone and Terrance turned to me, shocked, to say, "You're still taking those?" I was four months post-op. Many people would have already gone back to work, but the lab required me to pass a physical and be able to comfortably lift forty pounds. Terrance said that I shouldn't need them anymore. I discussed it with Ariel. She encouraged me that I could do it, that I was strong. We decided to throw the bottle away. I remember it feeling like I was throwing away a fresh slice of chocolate cake. But it was time. The next few days I didn't feel great, but it wasn't because of the pain. It was withdrawal.

What really truly helped me kick the habit was a support system. Without Ariel's love and encouragement, I don't know what would have happened. That is one of the biggest philosophies I hope we can instill in you. Find your support system. Lean on them. They will lift you up even when you falter. And support doesn't just have to mean friends and family. I was even getting support from my physical therapist Terrance.

During this time, I also started psychotherapy. It was incredibly helpful. It was a place where I could express all of the pressures that I felt and all the feelings of aimlessness. For anyone who is on the fence about therapy, it's great. It helped

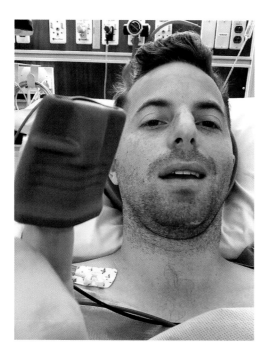

me feel like I could organize my brain again and lift the cloud.

Five years after that injury, I'd continued to experience a painful pop in my knee. Anytime I squatted down, there was a moment where my tendons lumped to one side all at once and it hurt a little. So, before my son, Wesley, was born last year, I elected to have an arthroscopic debridement and meniscectomy. It was a minor surgery that shaved down some of the scar tissue and removed damaged parts of my meniscus. I did this fully aware that

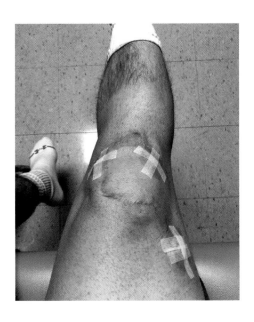

there would be a recovery period, fully aware that I was potentially risking going to a dark place *on purpose*. But if I didn't do it before we had the baby, when else could I spend a month focusing on my own body?

I did the surgery and, sure enough, afterward came the prescription for narcotics. Afterward came difficulty walking, the pain, the frustration. But this time I had been strengthening my mind and body for this event. If I had a bad day, I opened up to Ariel about it; I leaned on her support. I had built up muscle in my legs and thighs, so that they wouldn't atrophy as fast. I was aware of the risks of painkillers and took only very small doses and only when absolutely necessary. One week in, I didn't even need them anymore, so I flushed them down the toilet. I was fully committed to physical therapy exercises and went back to work within two weeks. At work I would even bust out resistance bands a few times a day and get in a quick PT sesh. I only had a few months before the baby's due date, so I was driven to get back into shape as quickly as possible.

Now I can play soccer again. I can squat with no pain. There's a slight degree of popping and I still get stiff through long movies or car rides, but it's much better. I'm better. And that's all I can hope for.

THE TRY GUYS LOOK BACK

I've always been insecure about the *American Ninja Warrior* Try Guys episode because I was set up to do something that needed incredible upper-body strength, and I knew I was just going to immediately fall in the water in front of a crowd and be embarrassed. It was a little bit by design for making a good video and creating some sort of victory for us as a group, but I certainly had the weakest performance, and every time we watched it back and everyone laughed at my immediate failure, it reminded me of my physical weakness. But we also watched dozens of highly skilled muscular people totally whiff it. I should be able to separate that in my mind, but it's easier said than done. We're our own harshest critics.

I don't think I've ever been more out of my element than when The Try Guys tried roller derby. For those who don't know, this is a sport in which buff women skate in circles on a banked track and basically knock the crap out of each other to get by. Now, any feeble man in my position—a complete novice going up against the L.A. Derby Dolls, the best women in the sport—would have reason to be scared. What if I added in that I didn't know how to roller skate? Yup.

So, the day before learning the physically punishing sport of roller derby, I first needed to master the gentle task of basic roller skating. A classic learn to walk before you run situation, but in this case the running was among a pack of bloodthirsty jungle cats. Now, old me would look at this and say *not a fucking chance, no thank you, good day, sirs and madams, korndiddy out!* But new me knows there's a video to be made, and I'm just gonna have to suck it up and jump right in. So we spent the day at a classic roller rink, and like a baby giraffe taking its first steps, I fumbled my way through learning to skate for the first time as a twenty-seven-year-old man with back problems. Did I say we spent the day? We spent an hour. What in the actual fuck.

Much to my horror, the first thing they teach you in roller derby is how to fall. It's not a question of *if* you're going to get knocked down, but rather *when*. And when you fall, you'd better fall right, or else you could break a bone or—and this made my skin crawl when I learned it—get a finger run over and chopped off. To learn how to play the sport, you first need to learn how to fall. Failing is written into the DNA of the sport. Everyone falls. What makes you win is your ability to get back up again. And, yeah, despite them telling me that it was no big deal, the idea of falling down still scared me. I'm a beautiful boy and I bruise easily.

Spoiler alert: I fell a lot. Early on, I fell right onto my tailbone, that bad fall they were trying to teach me to avoid. And yeah, it really hurt. And after an hour of falling repeatedly, the shock just melted away. It was my new normal, and it really wasn't so bad after all. Dare I say by the end of the day, falling was . . . fun? *It's fun.* Your adrenaline is pumping, you're flying around, knocking into people, and sure, you get knocked over. The thing I feared the most about this sport, the fear that held me back for so much of my childhood, ended up being the part I enjoyed the most!

And that seems to be true in everything I've encountered: your perception of the worst thing that can happen is always worse than reality.

Keith Tries Going Vegan: A ~~Dairy~~ Diary!

FOR ALL THE manboob-related reasons we've already discussed in this chapter, I've decided to try to go vegan! Do you realize how crazy that is? I am, like, the fried chicken God of my generation. Every day people tweet me pictures of fried chicken. They tag me in KFC tweets. They DM me fried chicken memes. I am, deservingly, an idol for fried chicken. I've even been hired by Sonic to do ads promoting their chicken tenders! Nobody wants to watch me "eat all the salads." People want to watch me eat fried chicken!

DAY 1

I didn't eat much. I had some cookies that didn't say explicitly that they were vegan but did appear to have no animal parts in the ingredient list. Maybe they snuck in horse hooves or something. For lunch I had a bland veggie burger from my favorite taco place. I don't mind that veggie burgers don't taste like burgers. I just want them to taste like *something*. For dinner I ate two and a half bowls of veggies that Becky lovingly made for us. As the best wife ever, she's decided to go vegan with me, and help hold me accountable. Swoon.

DAY 2

Breakfast was sad. Quinoa with fruit. It was just the most meh thing to start my day with. I also had a greens smoothie. I'm into them, even if they taste like plants. It's the best way to get greens into my body, so I've accepted that. Oh God I just realized that Caesar salad has anchovies in it! That will probably be the hardest part of it all. Learning about the secret animal dependence we all have.

DAY 3

Three days in and I'm already starting to get introspective about being vegan. You see, I'm known for being good at cooking meat. I have made Thanksgiving dinner for my friends and family for ten years. In my lifetime, I've made about 18 turkeys, 20 briskets, 50 pork shoulders, a dozen rib roasts, probably 1,000 steaks. Not that I'm counting or anything but I'm really good at it! I grew up believing that meat is the center of every lunch and dinner, and all the best breakfasts. I'm not bad at cooking vegetables, but I cook vegetables as a complement to the meat, not as the main event. I'm going to take this opportunity to learn how to make really flavorful vegan dishes that are actually healthy and use them for my and Becky's lunches.

DAY 5

Tonight was a big boys night. Let's just say boys nights tend not to skew vegan. We ended up eating late-night sushi and having cocktails at the top of a high-rise

downtown. I was definitely drunk, but when the sushi came I explained that I was vegan and would love some grilled vegetables if possible. I was transfixed on watching everyone else eat while I sucked edamame pods from their deliciously garlicky shells. They were really good. *Too good*. I was like "Wow! These pea pods are crushing it. Brian, you said these are garlic truffle oil, right? They're amazing . . ." And then it dawned on me ". . . do you think that it was truffle butter and not oil?"

Brian flipped through the menu and looked up at me with sad brown eyes. "Oh no. Yeah, it's butter. I won't tell anyone."

But I was crushed. I had worked so hard all week to avoid temptation. All undone by some stupid peapods drenched in stupid amazing butter that comes from stupid nonvegan cows. It was the first time that I messed up on this diet, and I felt duped.

DAY 6

Tonight Becky and I are meal prepping for the next few days, and also trying not to have excess because we are visiting family in Chicago this weekend. We also saw *Crazy Rich Asians* and I wanted to cry during the street food portion.

DAY 8

I made it a week! This is by far the longest I've ever gone in my life not eating meat/dairy/animal stuff. I wouldn't say I feel super different. I also don't think I look any different. I'm proud of myself for committing to it, but I don't know what I was expecting. The week has felt superlong, and maybe I'm realizing that the way to see results in this diet is to commit to it *forever*. Gosh, that seems so hard. Not just avoiding temptation at mealtime, but socially, all the time. Nobody envies a vegan. You may envy a vegan's health, but you don't envy their lifestyle. You pity them.

Day eight is also when my veganism goes head-to-head with my online character of Fried Chicken King. I am shooting a previously scheduled KFC "Eat the Menu" video for The Try Guys today, and I'm actually kind of afraid. I don't really want to do it. I don't want to reverse all the hard work I've put in this week with meal prepping and eating healthy.

Welp . . . after I went to town on the KFC, the bloating was pretty high. I was generally uncomfortable and really tired, quite irritable and with zero motivation. Something about how processed food is made more obviously bad when you eat a shit-ton of it. But digestion-wise, sadly it didn't really fuck me up too bad. I had a little constipation, but to my dismay, my body is really good at digesting this garbage, and I'm not proud of it. It's a reflection on my life of eating this way. It's a good lesson about this whole thing I'm trying to do. It takes more than a week to unlearn bad habits. It might even take years.

If I could reduce my meat/animal product consumption to only 5 percent of my diet, I think that would be a great, productive, reasonable change. Since we have roughly 21 meals a week, if one of my meals was all meat, or if two of my meals were centered on meat, that would be *so much better* than the life I've been living. Before this, I'd say that about 14 of my meals each week (all lunches and dinners) centered on meat, so 66 percent of my diet. Also, some of those meals are Korean barbecue, which is literally all beef and pork. This could also help with my social issue of having to eat vegan on a night out. It's just not an accommodation that all places can make, and the whole situation becomes stressful.

DAY 29

Yup, you read that right—I'm still vegan after a month, baby! It's hard, but I've seen improvements. I didn't go from flabby to fabulous, but I did go from flabby to slightly less flabby and slightly more fabulous. Full disclosure: I ate meat three times since KFC day so I'm not perfect! I thought I would cherish the opportunity to eat meat, but each time I took a bite, I was disappointed with the flavor and felt guilty that I'd undone a lot of positive work. That's so weird to say.

DAY 56

How impressed are you? You didn't think I could do it, did you? Well, to be honest, neither did I. I haven't had a steak in almost two months. I haven't had fried chicken since the KFC video. I *have* had a little bit of meat and other nonvegan food here and there because I think you need to set realistic goals. Also, the Vegan Bros told me that being 90 percent vegan is 100 times better than not being vegan at all. That math checks out. I'm not going to give up meat entirely, but I have become much more health conscious, and honestly, turned off by unhealthy options. Junk food isn't very appealing to me. I find myself craving interesting salads. I snack on handfuls of roasted nuts, popcorn, fruits, and veggies. Beef jerky is totally unappealing. Old Keith would slap me in the face just for saying that.

Since I tried CrossFit, I've also committed myself to exercising more. I couldn't convince Becky to try CrossFit with me but we've been doing Orangetheory Fitness, rowing, running, free weights, even a little Pilates. I would never have committed to it without Becky. Having someone to wake up with, get ready with, drive over with, and exercise with is so important. Neither of us can make an excuse not to go. Also, we're both looking better, our clothing is getting looser, our skin is getting healthier, and because we have to get up so early, we're drinking wine less in the evening.

EXPERT ADVICE FROM THE VEGAN BROS

MATT AND PHIL LETTEN
are vegan advocates and the authors of
Vodka Is Vegan. They're also bros and,
literally, brothers (there's a difference).

Here's their advice for those going vegan for the first time:

* To be clear, veganism is a plant-based diet that avoids all animal foods,
  like meat and fish, and animal products, like dairy and eggs.

* Find your "why." Remembering why you're doing this will keep you
  motivated. From the exploding lakes of shit (real thing; look it up), to
  fucked-up factory farms, or simply because you want to be healthy—
  the whys are endless. Just remember yours and it will be your guide.

* Swap it out. Replace that hamburger and sausage with the innovative
  plant-based versions from Beyond Meat. Switch out that chicken
  scaloppini with the vegan chick'n scaloppini from Gardein. Vegan food
  is getting so delicious, now even billionaires like Bill Gates and Richard
  Branson are investing.

* Remember that eating vegan is not an "all or nothing" proposition.
  Focus on progress over perfection. Chill the fuck out! Even vodka is
  vegan. Let's do a shot.

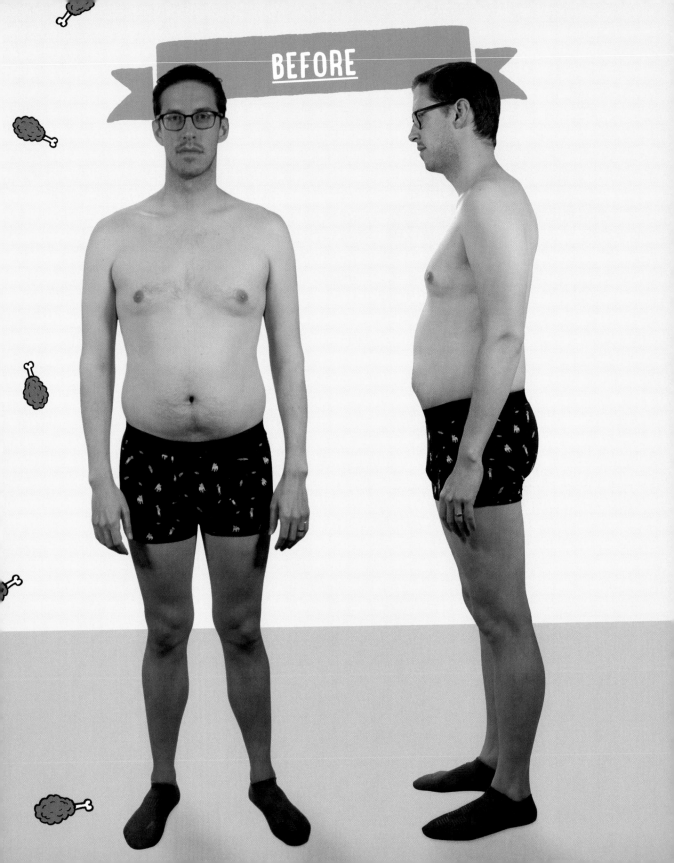

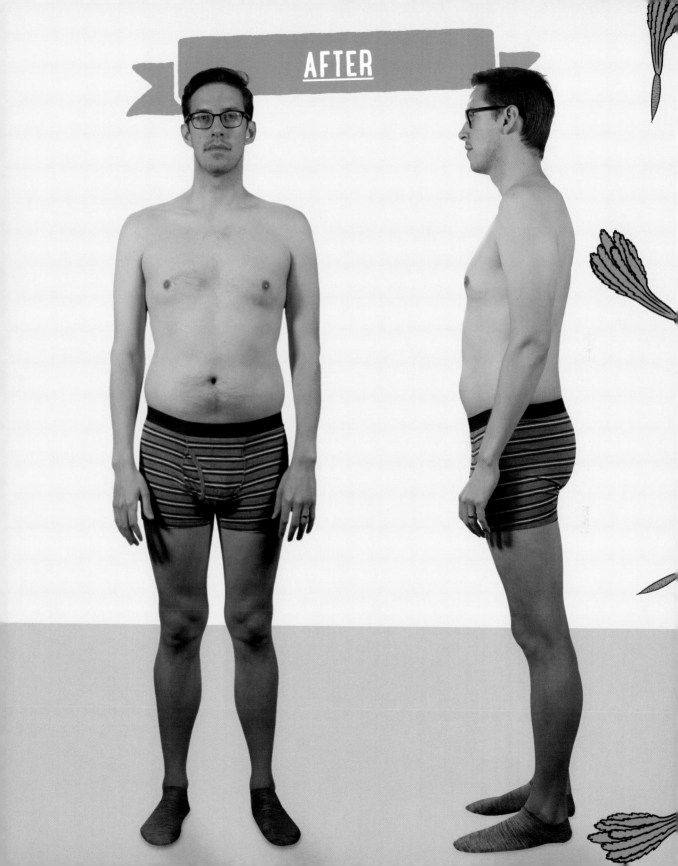

ONE HEALTHY CHOICE leads to another, and suddenly the unhealthy habits you were defending or afraid to leave behind are thoughts of the past, and you're excited about the improved person you are becoming. We aren't where we want to be yet, and where we want to be will always be changing. But we're trying, and though we're still losing little battles along the way, we're making more leaps forward than we ever have before.

I started this healthy journey because I was afraid that the bad habits I had would lead to sickness or even an early demise for good ol' Keith. But I've realized that change takes time. You have to do what you can. Change what you can. Try what you can. Be happy with the improvements you make, and strive to make more. At the end of the day it's all just habits. They aren't as hard to break as we think. And it's totally possible to make new, good ones!

I experienced a lot of judgment from people when I told them I was vegan, everything from "WHY?!" to "Oh, man, how long? I'm so sorry." It sucks that people who are doing something for the sake of their health feel like they are swimming upstream to do it. Each time I have to tell someone I'm vegan, I have some guilt about telling them, as if what I am doing is wrong when *it totally isn't*. I am starting to think that people who are wholly vegan are probably . . . right. It is healthier, and maybe the reason we think they're all so aggressive is actually that we're so aggressive toward *them*.

I'm not gonna stop eating fried chicken altogether, but I am going to stop eating *mostly* fried chicken altogether. After the first two months of veganism, I didn't have fried chicken for another whole month, and even then I had only one piece. This is huge for me.

And *believe me*, if I can do it, you can, too!

WHAT WE LEARNED

✳ Find a workout/diet buddy to share encouragement, accountability, and complaints with. You are only as a good as your support system!

✳ Paintball is a serious contact sport, *Ned*.

✳ Listen to your body, even if other people, including doctors, tell you nothing is wrong. You know yourself better than anybody.

✳ The most powerful weapon against a bad habit is a good habit.

CHAPTER THREE

Style

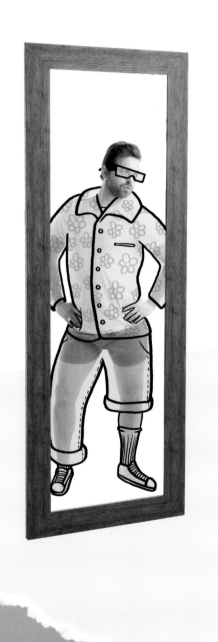

It's what's inside that counts."

"Don't judge a book by its cover."

"Always wear clean underwear."

We all know these are bullshit rules. If they were true, nobody would care about fashion, everyone would be dressed in garbage bags, and Forever 21 would cease to exist, leaving a hole in the hearts of millennial girls everywhere (and Zach*).

To most of us "style" is just another word for clothes, but nay. Nay, we say! Your style and image are the crux of how you are perceived and presented to the world. We're visual beings, and our impressions of people are largely informed by what we see. It's a somewhat unfortunate reality, but the way you look—and by extension, how you dress—plays a tremendous role in how others interact with you. It touches upon every facet of life, from attraction all the way to who will hire you. That can be incredibly overwhelming.

When you're picking an OOTD, it pays to have a good eye, deep pockets, and no fear. Unfortunately, we don't have any of those (except Eugene). The rest of us have fucked up nearly every lewk we've tried to pull off in our short, sartorially challenged lives. But lucky for you, we kept receipts and want to walk you through our catwalk of failures. And, lucky for us, since we still have those receipts, we will be returning half the crazy shit we bought for this chapter.

---

* For real, I love F21.

What's Wrong with Us

I'VE ALWAYS HAD a deep insecurity about my clothes. To this day, when I look in my closet I get a dreadful, sinking feeling. Ugh. Clothes that I once loved start to feel stale. None of the outfits ever seem to fit together. Never one for making dramatic decisions in the morning, I end up gravitating toward my comfort zone: solid-color polo shirts or T-shirts, dark blue jeans, casual brown shoes. And off I go into an anonymous workforce of hip, creative professionals.

It wasn't always this way. When I was a kid, I put on clothes without a second thought for how it looked, made easier in that my style consisted of whatever my mom bought for me. I don't ever recall thinking about what to wear or not to wear; I was more concerned with playing touch football than projecting an image.

Things changed around middle school. Isn't that always the age? Other kids would make negative comments about my outfits that profoundly affected me. Since it was the 1990s, most of the choice phrases included "gay." Still wearing tighty whities? "Dude. That's so gay." Your shorts are too short? "OMG. You look so gay." (Did kids say "OMG" in the 1990s? Let's go with yes.) If I knew then what I know now about how "gay" actually means fabulously stylish, I would have taken it as a compliment. But this was 1997. I was ten and I was mortified.

I remember one afternoon coming home to my mom in tears because my shorts had gotten

insulted so badly. They were simple shorts. Probably red because it rhymes with Ned. Possibly pleated. Riding a little shorter than the typical cool boys' hemline at that time, which was just below the knee. I sobbed to my mother that my clothes weren't cool. And clearly, I knew what cool was. Cool was Gap cargo pants and long sleeve T-shirts. Cool was Abercrombie & Fitch gear with writing on it that told you when the store was "Est." Cool was Joe Boxers with the waistline showing. Cool was an L.L.Bean backpack with your initials on it. Cool was everything I was made fun of for not having.

Cool was not pleated shorts from a department store.

To cheer me up, my mom took me on a clothes shopping spree that week. Gap. Old Navy . . . well, only Gap and Old Navy, actually. I remember thinking it was so awesome that I finally had cargo shorts. Finally I could put extra things in massive pockets on my thighs. What I needed to carry around at age ten (yo-yos?), I have no idea. I remember trashing all my tighty whities and converting to wearing boxers exclusively (at this time, I had not yet discovered the magic of boxer briefs). It was glorious.

Looking back as an adult, I realize that I wasn't becoming more stylish, I was merely conforming to what most middle school boys from Jacksonville, Florida, were wearing in 1997. I was saying I see other people in my school wearing this, and therefore I will probably get made fun of less. I may have rationalized this by thinking that I wanted people to like me for my personality and my humor rather than my clothes. The truth is that I was, and still am, afraid that someone is going to judge me. Afraid that I'll be too "out there."

When I met my wife, Ariel, she provided me with boundless encouragement. "Those look great on you!" she would say, or "I love that color." What was once a swirling well of confusion about what to wear became a fountain of positivity and I gained more confidence in my outward appearance. I felt attractive.

But I was still secretly judging people who wore flashy outfits. For example, one of the first times I saw Eugene at BuzzFeed's office, he was wearing a suit and tie. BuzzFeed was a casual place back then, and most people came to work in T-shirts and jeans. I remember thinking to myself, "Who does this guy think he is? This is not a formal event. This is a chill media company. Is he trying to impress somebody?" The fact that he was so overdressed made me almost . . . angry? But why? Why should I care? Maybe I was actually envious of his *attitude*, the carefree nonchalance with which he moved through the office despite wearing a ridiculously impractical suit for an intern. If he cared about what people thought, he hardly showed it. And that was something I yearned to do myself.

I'VE UNDERGONE a bit of a personal style renaissance over the past few years—some might even call it a glow-up—and it's had ripple effects throughout my life. Admittedly, from where I was starting I could only go up. Eugene will be the first to jump out and take full credit for the fact that we now dress better . . . and, yeah, that's probably true. That dude even manages to make sweatpants look cool. While I certainly can't give Eugene *full credit* for my

improved style, having a fashionable friend rubs off on you. We could probably just skip this whole chapter and sum it up with "go shopping with your cool, trendy gay friends." But that would be playing into stereotypes and we don't stand for that here. Plus, I'll have you know I have several gay friends who dress totally stupid.

When I met the other guys, I was hopelessly trapped in postcollege-lazy-stoner-straight-dude chic. I wore zip-up hoodies basically all day, every day as the only semblance of layers I owned. I thought my thick-rimmed glasses were supertrendy and cute but now I realize they totally obscured my face and really did me no favors. And holy shit I wore the ugliest black exercise sneakers as my only pair of shoes. I shudder looking back at old photos. But, sure, let's print them in a book to exist forever and ever. Great.

I want to give myself a little credit here, though, because I wasn't totally clueless in how I dressed. I just had no idea how to combine the few good ideas I did have into stylish looks. I have always used clothes as a way to appear more outgoing and as a way to express my rampant individuality. I'm not going to try to convince you that I've looked good all my life, but I wasn't just your regular sheep falling into line and conforming. The world needed to know, and I used my most outward expression to set myself apart. As my previous outfits will loudly tell you, just because you're trying to look unique doesn't mean you look good.

Some of you may know people who dress like I did, or maybe you dress like I did. There's nothing wrong with that! If you're happy and confident with how you dress, then go off and conquer this world and feel free to use these pages to practice some doodles (I like giving Keith a mustache). That wasn't my experience, though. I didn't like the way I dressed because I didn't like the version of me it was projecting. I felt like there was someone better underneath the surface and I just lacked the tools to unearth him. It kept people from taking me seriously at work. It made me look and feel like a kid instead of an adult. I can only imagine that it's part of why I struggled in dating for so long.

 I'VE NEVER BEEN one to choose to be fashionable. It's been something other people have tried to help me with. I enjoy looking good, but if I walk out of the house just looking okay, that's fine with me for the most part. To be fully fashionable every day just doesn't seem necessary, you know? The longest I've ever gone dressing cool, or maybe just with the intent to be cool, is probably three to four days, and it has always been correlated with a convention or an event. I tend to stick with the rule of "Do I think someone will see me today?" If the answer is no then I'll wear an old Try Guys shirt and jeans. . . .

 Yes, those are the best days. If I think someone will see me, I get stressed out in the morning.

 THIS PHOTO ABOVE was taken by Eugene, who as I write this is also dressed for a day where no one will see him. . . .

See! Even his lounging around clothes are cool! It's relaxed, but it's still an outfit. Also just look how serious he is. *Swoon.*

The worst outfit I ever wore was in junior high. My friend Hank and I decided we wanted to dress as outrageously as possible, and so we wore turtlenecks under Hawaiian shirts and then added terrible ties. Like Pillsbury Doughboy ties. Sure, it was a way to defy the fashion standards of the popular kids, who wore Hollister and Abercrombie & Fitch, but it also just made us laugh.

After that phase, I turned to Hot Topic, which was all the rage, so that I could wear shirts with jokes and opinions on my chest. I enjoyed those shirts because they invited people to remark on them, which initiated conversations. Granted, they were mostly remarks like, "What's that supposed to mean?"

Here's one of my favorites:

Honestly, I have no idea what that's supposed to mean. *Was it calling people dogs? Calling people bitches?* No clue, but it made a lot of people talk to me, which is mostly what I wanted out of life at that time.

"Dad to the bone."

 "Zach is my favorite Try Guy."

 "I hate shirts with text on them."

I'M HYPERCONSCIOUS about the projection of my image and I'm known to be the most fashionable and stylish of The Try Guys. I've always seen it as an important mode of expression; my unique upbringing conditioned me to accept that looks are not only important, they're absolutely vital.

In Korean culture, having beauty and style could mean the difference between you and another candidate for a prime job or desirable suitor. Since my parents were immigrants and we were the only Asian family in our town for a good amount of my childhood, my mother took the reins on the one thing she could undeniably control: the way my sisters and I dressed. We weren't well-off by any means, but we faked affluence by scouring the discount bins at Neiman Marcus's off-brand department stores and scooping up any used item featuring a designer label. In middle school, when a new friend of mine came home for a playdate after swimming practice, I was surprised to see his face crinkle in confusion when we arrived at our modest little home. "I thought y'all were loaded," he said innocently. "Y'all always look so put together." My mom's plan had worked.

My mom would later tell me that she was in constant fear that I'd be bullied for being Asian (which I was), so she was determined to make sure there wasn't any added fuel for my tormentors be-

cause of how I dressed. Some interesting insight into the reasoning behind one of her more stringent rules that infuriated me as a child: we weren't allowed to play video games, which she often fibbed would give us "thumb cancer." I assumed it was because she'd rather I focused on studying, but when I was older she would confess that she had seen her friends' children get sucked into obsessing over Warcraft and GoldenEye and they looked and sounded "like nerds." She refused to allow me to develop any habits that would threaten the image she so carefully cultivated. No son of hers would be a nerd.

To have significant emphasis put on your face, your hair, your dress, your shoes, your posture, your body—everything—and how it equates to your future success will inevitably make you vain. Riddled with insecurity and self-hatred, yes, but still, my sisters and I implicitly understood that when something looked nicer, it was "better." I enjoyed being fashionable and embraced it as a distinct form of expression, something that was extremely important to me as I grew more comfortable in my queer identity, which occupied a huge part of my focus and evolution in my college years and twenties.

Icon in Training

AS IS UNFORTUNATELY TRUE with most things in my life, I didn't change until I was forced to. The impetus? Seeing myself on camera for the first time. For those who have never filmed themselves, let me be the first to tell you that being on camera is, on the whole, a humiliating experience. To be filmed is an

A BRIEF HISTORY OF TRYING

Björk wore an insane swan dress to the 2001 Oscars.
On one hand, *weird*. On the other hand, *icon*.

inherently vulnerable undertaking, and if you're anything like me and are already your own worst critic, turning a camera on yourself is the perfect opportunity for self-judgment and shame.

Over the course of my first year at BuzzFeed it became a cruel, unwritten rule: any day you dressed cute, no one would be filming anything. Any day you looked like absolute shit, you'd get pulled into a video that would blow up and get millions of views. Again and again my worst looks were captured and cemented on the internet forever. There's only so much a man can take. And whatever they can take, I can take half of.

Our third video together, "Guys Recreate Kim Kardashian's Butt Photo," was filmed spontaneously. It's one of the biggest videos we've ever made and I cannot stand watching it because of how stupid I look. I filmed some sort of exercise video earlier that day, so in the Kim K. video my hair is flattened from sweat and I'm wearing oversize basketball shorts. I'm forgettable at best. I vowed on that day—sometime between oiling Keith's butt and falling asleep at 4 a.m. after a lengthy shower—that I would reform my style. I had to.

Change did not come overnight. It started with admitting that I wanted to change, first to myself, then to the world. The world responded. One of my closest friends, Ashly, told me she loved shopping but hated spending money. I loved spending money but hated shopping! We were a match made in heaven. In exchange for free coffees, she agreed to be my shopping buddy and personal stylist, joining me on weekend shopping trips whenever we were bored and instilling me with the confidence to try new things. Whenever I was unsure of something, my friend was there to give me a boost, cheering me on. It ended up being just the nudge I needed.

One of the first huge lessons I learned is to not just go out and buy things you already own. We all fall into this trap; early on in my shopping experience, I'd excitedly hurry back to Ashly, pounds of clothes draped over my arms, only to be met with a disapproving frown.

"What are you doing? Look down."

And sure enough, all the clothes I'd gravitated to were just close siblings of

the things I already owned or was currently wearing. There's a fine line between having an aesthetic and lacking the mettle to try something new.

Change is always scary, and even something as simple as the difference between a polo and a Henley (polo's sexier British cousin) can really throw you for a loop. I'd pretty comfortably carved out a little cozy niche and knew that staying there, while not enhancing my life, would at least serve to shield me from ever really making a fool of myself (at least as far as wardrobe goes). Despite my objections, we put back every button-down and instead went looking for more interesting alternatives—still me, but inching toward the unknown. When we got home, I may or may not have thrown a little fit (I'm so sorry, Ashly), and it took literally photographing myself in different clothing combinations to feel comfortable and confident in some of my new looks. It was basically like using Pinterest, but instead of pins of fashionable men it was me with a forced smile standing in front of my dirty closet. I used those pictures for the first two weeks every morning when I got dressed, and soon after I'd internalized enough for it to suddenly feel natural. You know what? On second thought, maybe Ashly deserved more than free coffee for all this nonsense.

Here's another fun tip that can trick you into dressing better: buy something way cooler than anything else you own and you'll be forced to up the game of the rest of your wardrobe. When Kanye West announced he was dropping the Yeezy Boost 350 sneakers for the first time, the fashion world creamed their collective pants. It was still pretty early on in my fashion renaissance and I had no idea what Yeezys were or why I should care (now that I'm more educated, I'm even less sure). Through a series of events not worth detailing, I found myself owning a pair. It felt amazing. They were the coolest wearable thing I had ever owned by far, and they seemed to make even my dumbest outfits look cooler. I was getting compliments just walking down the street. Can you imagine?

But about three days in, I realized I couldn't just keep wearing them every day or else they'd lose their luster, both figuratively from overexposure and literally from wear. So I went out and bought more sneakers just to balance my rotation. And then some new pants to complement the shoes. And a new jacket that I thought would look nice with its speckled design. My sneakers inspired some new outfits, which meant I got to go shopping even more. One pair of shoes ended up totally revolutionizing my closet. By the end, the Yeezys were the least favorite thing I owned (plus Kanye did some real questionable shit and I started feeling weird about wearing them). As they say, a rising tide raises all the sneakers. That's the saying, right?

Best Use for a Man Bag Ever (Wait for It . . .)

OF COURSE, I used to dress just horribly. I was a shitty T-shirt and cargo pants kinda guy. Like a lazily designed Dance Dance Revolution character or a teenage stoner on a network sitcom. By the way, what is with The Try Guys and cargo pants? I dunno. But then my wife, Becky, came along and implemented what I call fashion waves Alpha and Bravo. Military terms are appropriate due to the gravity of the situation here. Wave Alpha was getting me into gingham and plaid button-downs and jeans. But since I tend to live in the one thing I think works, I just only bought the same type of shirt for the next four years, until my closet resembled that of a cartoon character. Shirts with blue squares became part of my identity.

Wave Bravo was getting into more colors, and sweaters and cardigans. *That* phase started only last year. Wave Charlie is classified top-secret but let's just say it involves a lot of leather.

Sometimes I look at my closet and say, "I'll dress shitty today because I want to wear that cool shirt tomorrow." But why don't I just have lots of clothes that I like so that I can dress cool every day? If the other things I have done for this book have taught me anything, it's that to fully change yourself in a way that sticks, you gotta make the new way of life a habit. It's not enough to do something for a week . . . you gotta do it for a month or two and really try to make it the new normal.

I recently had to find a fun look for a video I'm shooting, so I went shopping for something "autumnal" with my friend Jared Popkin, who loves shopping. I do not, obviously, but maybe that's because half the time I am trying to help Becky find something she likes, and I don't feel like I am a good helper, and then the other half of the time I am going after work, so I have like half an hour to find an outfit for something and I am super stressed and pressured into buying the first thing I see.

But this trip was different. It was casual, and I had a friend to constantly bounce ideas and opinions off. It was like having a workout buddy, if a workout lasted four hours and ended in margaritas. We even found a great look for which I ended up getting final approval from The Try Guys.

It was nice to get sweet comments from the boys about it. I think it helps me to break out of my comfort zone. Like Ned, I just have this fear of looking stupid out in public because the outfit is foreign to me, and I don't have the confidence to pull it off. In fact, just like Ned on day five of his fashion fears try (more on that later), I recently had to wear a chest bag for one of our videos. I think it's technically called a cross body, but let's not get it twisted, people: it's basically a fanny pack you wear on your chest.

As soon as I put it on and started walking through the mall I got *so insecure*. Maybe it was because I talked so much shit about them before I put it on that I as-

EXPERT ADVICE FROM ARIEL FULMER

ARIEL is an interior designer and stylist working in Los Angeles. She is the owner of styling firm Fig + Stone Designs and an avid collector of vintage furniture and decor. She also happens to be Ned's lovely wife!

Here are her top tips for showcasing your style at home:

✳ **GOOD DESIGN DOESN'T HAVE TO BE EXPENSIVE.** Interior design is like fashion for your house. And like fashion, it's not about how much you spend, it's about how you use it. I often mix high-end furniture with pieces from places like Ikea and CB2.

✳ **MIX IT UP.** Many people think a well-designed home should look like a catalog and that's just not true. Most of the time you don't wear an entire outfit from one store, so why would you buy all your furniture from one place? The general rule is no more than three items of furniture from one store.

✳ **TAKE CHANCES ON SEASONAL ITEMS.** Like your closet, you should have a few good neutral items that will stand the test of time, but smaller items like pillows and ceramics are a great way to bring in bright colors and fun patterns that might go out of season.

✳ **MESS THINGS UP!** Life is messy and a home should look and feel like a place you live—like your favorite pair of jeans. As a stylist I like to incorporate personal items and funky vintage pieces to give a space some life.

sumed everyone hated them. I just felt so embarrassed even though it was totally unjustified. In reality, I got zero weird looks, and when I met up with a friend, he just said, "Neat bag, when did you get that?" He didn't even have a negative opinion of it, but I immediately said, *"It's for a video I don't know how I feeeeeellll."*

But then I learned true happiness when I helped him sneak a burger into the movie in the little pouch. That should really be part of the marketing . . .

Fashion Pokémon

GAY CULTURE HAS a toxic, often brilliant connection with my Korean background, gifting me with years of beating myself up over every pimple, every iota of fat, every single shirt I would wear and what it would say about me as a fiercely independent queer person of color. The pressure to align your looks with your voice was set high by my mother and then launched into the stratosphere by the LGBT community. Always remember that anyone whose outfit or hairstyle impresses you has despaired much longer and harder about how to make it all appear effortless than you would otherwise assume.

However, the agony behind the reasons why I might focus on my outer presentation pales in comparison to the glory of truly coming into my own and dressing in ways that more accurately reflect my inner character. My dramatic style evolution, much like an ever-changing, fantastical Pokémon, was less of an "adding on" ex-

perience and more of a "stripping away" revelation. Wardrobe, hairstyles, makeup—they might appear more cultivated and crafted, but in truth, I feel most comfortable when strangers can meet the dazzling, gregarious, fabulous personality that resides within my sometimes steely veneer just by looking at what I'm wearing. I've learned how to literally wear my culture and soul on my sleeve. I'm realizing so many new and exciting versions of my final form.

As I become more open and in touch with the charming, effervescent entertainer that I've always been but was too frightened and psychologically damaged to flaunt, my styling, especially at public events, has shifted as well. When I wear a skirt or lipstick or heels, it automatically starts a conversation with passersby who don't once have to question my sexuality, which is a freeing experience for an LGBT person. They skip an entire step in the typical dialogue and I can immediately launch into my deepest, truest personality: a fierce, hilarious, engaging diva. And if someone judges me for how I appear, I instantly know that I do not need to ever associate with that asshole again. Fashion, for queer people,

can be a constant, beautiful coming-out moment, and even though the emotions behind our community's struggle might be tinged with darkness, there is no better remedy than genuinely feelin' yourself in a look that both stuns the crowd and represents you at your best and most honest.

Many young readers are also fabulous, mythical creatures but might not be sharing that sensational energy with the world yet. Don't worry; it takes time, confidence, acceptance, and a devil-may-care attitude that should also be balanced with an environment where it is safe to express yourself. Just know that I, a queer person of color who hated himself and had no outlets to properly showcase the sheer breadth of my amazingness as a child, evolved into a magical fucking unicorn.

No Regrets

THERE'S NO DENYING I look better now. It's my clothes, it's my hair, and really it's just my overall demeanor. I can't say for certain that dressing better has made me a better person, but it certainly correlates to a lot of positive changes in my life. Once I started dressing better, I became more confident both in videos and in real life, and I found myself being taken more seriously as a professional. It's pretty impossible to separate my growth in style and my growth as a person, because they've been one and the same.

Even now, post-glow-up, I have days where I just can't be bothered to think about my outfits. The reality is that you'll never stop having those days. Even models (aka me) need days to wear their favorite oversize sweater, skip shaving, and bum around in a dad hat. The key is to slowly upgrade your pieces so that even your fallback, don't-think-about-it outfits

have a coherence to them. You don't have to be "on trend" to look good; you just need to be put together and trick others into thinking you know what you're doing. It's all a big mental game. The obvious should also be stated that it's still a work in progress and I continue to whiff on outfits all the time.

It's possible I'll look back at myself in a few years and think current me dresses like an idiot. In truth, I've never once looked back at old photos and thought to myself: "Yeah, that guy gets it." When I was eight, I begged my mom to buy me JNCOs—preposterously oversize baggy jeans, first made popular by 1990s skating culture and rappers and later by fans of the musical group Insane Clown Posse. I absolutely had to have a pair. After weeks of me pleading and arguing the utmost social importance of owning them, my mom finally agreed, but only

on the condition that we do a photo shoot to prove to my future self just how stupid I looked. So one day, fresh from a shower, I jumped into my pants and confidently struck some fuego poses in the backyard. I think the photos speak for themselves. Look who's laughing now, Mom.

The process of evolving your style is never over. What works today will look stupid tomorrow. And if that's the case, you're even more free to throw caution to the wind and do whatever the fuck you want. Once you realize that it's all a ruse, you'll realize that no one actually knows what the fuck they're doing. You just need to do what makes you feel awesome. In that, it's also beneficial to dig your feet down and have a personal style that you feel good in, that's resistant to trends. You don't need to go changing who you are every year. Permit yourself to look stupid and dare to experiment. Wear your clothes as a badge of expression instead of as a comfort blanket. If you project an image of confidence and power, the world will treat you accordingly.

Think like a queen. A queen is not afraid to fail.
Failure is another stepping-stone
to greatness.

—*Oprah fucking Winfrey*

Ned Tries to Face His Fashion Fears!

I'M READY! After consulting with an expert, each day for a week I'm going to wear an outfit that includes several elements that terrify me. And then I'm going to live my life like I normally do—go to work, go out to lunch—without ever taking off the outfit. I'm going to see how I feel about the clothes and how the world feels about me. It's time to stop being so safe and start taking some chances!

~ DAY 1 ~

DAY 1

FASHION FEAR: Patterns

DEGREE OF ANXIETY: Mild

OUTFIT:

* Plaid overcoat (Topman)
* Seventies diamond collared shirt (Topman)
* Black and white plaid pants (Topman)
* Black leather oxford shoes (Topman)

THIS IS MY FIRST DAY exclusively wearing outfits that my stylist, Roman, picked out for me. I stayed home until 10:30 a.m. because I really didn't want to put on these clothes. And because I felt cozy in gym shorts. I know that these clothes are supposed to be cool and exciting, but I am not looking forward to the prospect of wearing them today. I guess I just gotta suck it up.

I do not like mixing crazy patterns. I always just feel like I'm going to mess it up or it's going to be too out there. Too *loud*. I'll wear plaid occasionally, but I've never done diamonds, plaid, and another type of plaid all at once. But there are people out there who wear these types of outfits every day. I'm imagining what people are going to think and I keep dreading that I'll be seen as a fraud. "Oh, there he is. Mr. Dad trying to be cool."

First thing I will say upon getting dressed, though, is that I feel like I need a bag that matches this outfit, as opposed to the regular old backpack I take to work. I need a brown leather bag or something. Ooh, maybe an attaché case! It's crazy, wearing interesting clothing has already made me think more critically about all other aspects of my appearance. I'm thinking, "How am I going to do my hair? What sort of sunglasses am I going to wear? Does my backpack match my outfit?" I have literally never thought "Does my backpack match my outfit?" in my whole life! (Spoiler alert: it does not.)

Time to head to work and see what the guys think . . .

regular old
backpack

 I like this a lot. Love the patterns. I'd maybe replace the backpack.

 That's what I said!

 This would actually look good with *my* backpack.

 That tracks. Took me about an hour to get dressed.

 Why?

 Mostly I just procrastinated.

 Yeah, you're a bum.

 Eugene's approval is huge since he's the resident fashion aficionado, obviously. I need to do work but with this outfit on I feel like I shouldn't be working at a computer. I should be drinking a glass of whiskey. What do you say, Zach?

 First of all, I came in and I said, "Whoa." And then I said, "Oh my God." And then I said, "I know this shirt." Because I almost bought this shirt. Is this Topshop or is it Zara?

 Topshop. Oh God. I'm dressed like Zach Kornfeld's wet dream right now.

There are so many patterns. It's like an assault on my eyes. Yeah, I don't know that I could say that this is a good outfit, frankly.

 Thanks, Zach, I'm gonna go cry in the bathroom now.

 I think it's a fantastic outfit. I think it's sexy as fuck. I'd wear this. It's so dope.

 I love the pieces, I guess.

 One of you I trust way more when it comes to fashion.

 The patterns are tight enough where, especially from a distance, it looks like you're just wearing like maybe even just a basic print. When you get closer it looks like there's more complexity, but I don't get turned off by the patterns.

 Just know that everything you say I'm hyperanalyzing and will think about as I fall asleep tonight.

 Your outfit feels like you took a music visualizer and just played dubstep all at once. I'll say I've never seen you dressed like this and I'm excited.

 Thank you. Well, just you wait, this was the outfit that I felt the most comfortable in.

 Oh, man, this is the easing in?

 This is just Monday's outfit. You know what they say? Make vids, drink coffee, make money.

 Tell me you're not on your way to a swingers party right now.

 Maybe.

 Yeah. This is a sex-stuff outfit.

TODAY I GOT a lot of compliments but also a few jabs at my outfit. How did that make me feel? Not great. You can get ten compliments, but if you get one negative thing said about you, that's the one you always remember. Same with YouTube comments. I gotta stop reading those.

Ariel didn't get to see my outfit before she left this morning, because of my procrastination. But when I got home, she loved the outfit! She wanted the coat for herself, actually. So that's . . . a good thing? All in all, it was a successful first day. I learned that the key to matching patterns is that they need to be similar and of a similar color palette. And then you can pretty much do *anything*. But I can't wait to put on sweatpants.

DAY 2

FASHION FEAR: Jean jackets, funky sunglasses

DEGREE OF ANXIETY: Mild

OUTFIT:

* Fashion sunglasses (Roman's closet)
* Jean jacket (Calvin Klein)
* Plaid shirt (Patagonia)
* White pants (Gap)
* Brown dress shoes (Cole Haan)

DAY 2'S LEWK actually came from my closet, mostly. My own white pants, which I've only worn twice. My jean jacket, which I could never bring my-self to wear even once. The sunglasses are from Roman, and I would never wear them normally. Ariel said I kinda look like Bono, and then specified that that's a good thing. I mean, he is a billionaire.

Today I'm picking Keith up to drive across town for a very important meeting and he has no idea I'm going to be dressed like this.

~ DAY 2 ~

Are you wearing fashion glasses?

 Yes, sir.

 Wow. Eugene's going to be jealous.

 That's the whole reason I'm doing this.

 You'll be doing all the talking in the meeting today. I dare not speak.

 I still don't know if I have the confidence to wear the glasses in the meeting.

 It makes much more sense why you're late now.

 It took me forty-five minutes to get dressed. I thought about wearing normal clothes to this meeting and then I was like, "You know what? An important, fancy meeting is *exactly* the time when you wear something a little out there."

 Flashy.

 Yup. I'm sorry that we're running late. But when you dress like this, you don't have to be on time.

 I DID END UP taking off the glasses for the meeting because I'm not a total maniac. But to be honest, I felt empowered in this outfit today. It was also a very stark reminder that I *already* have some daring clothes in my closet that I can make work if I just step outside my comfort zone a little. I don't know why I never wore that jean jacket before. Totally something I could have pulled off. Now I love it.

I guess what I'm saying is, fashion starts *right here*. (I'm pointing to my heart.)

EXPERT ADVICE FROM ROMAN SIPÉ

FASHION STYLIST ROMAN SIPÉ is widely known in the industry for his men's editorial work. The primary focus of his career has been to express his own vision of men and to transform the perceptions of what is considered acceptable in men's fashion. He's basically the coolest guy we know.

Here are his tips for facing your fashion fears:

* **TAILORING:** People tend to look at photos of celebs or models and think, "I love that outfit, but it's not going to look like that on me." However, you'd be amazed at how different things look and feel when they're tailored to fit your body.

* **ONE PIECE AT A TIME:** If you have an idea of an outfit you want to try but fear it's too outlandish in comparison to your current style, just ease your way into it. Break it down and gradually introduce new things into your wardrobe one piece at a time.

* **STYLISH FRIENDS:** If you fear standing out too much in an outfit, call up your most fashionable friend and hang out with them for a day. They are likely to give you the most positive feedback and be excited that you are taking steps to enhance your style. Plus, all of the focus will no longer be on you. The people you choose to spend your time with have a huge impact on your actions, behaviors, and mind-set.

* **BE CONFIDENT:** Even if you aren't completely confident in an outfit, the key is to at least act like you are. Keep those shoulders pulled back, chest high, and smile no matter what. Your confidence will build as you start to improve your style from the inside out!

~ DAY 3 ~

DAY 3

FASHION FEAR: Crop tops, jewelry

DEGREE OF ANXIETY: Moderate

OUTFIT:

* Silver necklace (H&M)
* Black crop T-shirt (Zara Women's)
* Black wash denim jeans (Gap)
* Chelsea boot (Topman)

DAY 3 and it's come to this. I'm wearing a fucking crop top! But I've stopped procrastinating in the morning and just got dressed so Ariel had a chance to comment on my outfit before anyone else saw me. She wasn't thrilled with my jewelry but she did think the crop top was "bitchin'." She wants to keep it, too. Damn. Ariel is stealing all my looks.

We also had a lengthy conversation about my belly, which I'm going to have to keep sucked in all day—on official orders from Roman. Ironically, my muffintop only comes out when I stand up. When I sit down this just becomes a regular shirt. Ariel thinks I should just let it all hang out, even if I only have a single strip of belly hair.

The ironic thing is, in the three days I've been facing my fashion fears, it's gone from blazing hot in LA and me wearing an overcoat, to superchilly and now I'm in a crop top. Ariel offered to let me wear her cardigan in case I got cold. Silly Ariel. A cardigan would never go with this outfit.

And now, off to work.

Boop.

 Don't touch my belly, please. We still don't have an HR department.

 Your necklace is very Illuminati, if I'm being honest. It's like a triangle with an eyeball.

 I can't wait until Eugene gets here. He's going to be like, "You stole my outfit."

 Oh, yeah. He's going to be dressed in the same thing.

 My stomach's already getting tired. This is from the women's section of Zara, by the way. It adds a little pop of skin but not too much to be scandalous.

 Wait. I'm wearing black on black right now, too.

 But I've got a crop top.

 What is exciting me most about this moment is like, "The way I dressed myself is the way that Roman dressed someone else?"

 Exactly. Pretty much. The only other thing is a little jewelry.

 I always want jewelry. I just don't know where to get it.

 H&M.

 How about that.

 So, what do you think, Eugene?

 I love it. I'm a big crop top fan. You know what? I might like every single one of these outfits just because I like pushing fashion boundaries. It's a subtle crop top. It's not all the way up to here.

Just a little bit of my hair showing.

 Crop tops originally were like worn by dudes in the 1980s who were athletes.

 Oh?

 Remember? It was very big in the 1980s, so, yeah. This almost looks like you're about to go—I don't know, lift some weights, bro.

 Yeah, brah. Get huge, brah. Get huge.

 I like it.

 Also, you'll really like this touch. For the first time ever, I'm wearing a necklace.

 I wear necklaces a lot.

 I know you do.

 It's good, though. I'm into it. I'm glad the jeans are skinny. But it is still very Ned because there's a belt. If you're going to wear a skirt or something next, then that's what I want to see for sure.

 Oh, you just wait.

 I KINDA LIKED the crop top today. It was certainly a conversation piece and it forced me to keep my stomach tucked in all day, which was difficult. There were actually a few women in the office today also wearing crop tops. We became belly buddies. I could see myself wearing this again . . . no joke. It takes a lot of confidence to dress like this when you have a dad bod, and there's nothing wrong with a little confidence in my life.

STYLE

DAY 4

FASHION FEAR: See-through, lace, earrings, big hat

DEGREE OF ANXIETY: Extreme

OUTFIT:

* Hat (Roman's personal collection)
* Silver hoop earrings (Roman's personal collection)
* Lace shirt (Menagerie)
* Silk shorts (Menagerie)
* Tux shoes (Topman)

 COME ON, things are getting insane. Ariel thinks I look like a rogue Boy Scout. I asked her if she could see my nipples and she replied, "That's the *first* thing I saw!" But she also said that if we didn't know each other and she saw me in the street, we would not be dating, but I could be her gay best friend. She also said she was worried that my nipples would chafe in the chilly weather later. Then I hugged her and almost blinded her with the brim of my hat.

Today's gonna be an interesting day. First to the office and then to a Rams football game while. Still. Wearing. This. Outfit. Here we go!

 When would you wear this and it be appropriate? Like, is it a festival look? Maybe it's a goth club look.

 I mean, I like the shirt. Roman is very into those shirts. He's tried to get me to wear them several times, and I'm like, body hair don't work with that.

You kinda look like a witch.

What do you guys think of the earrings?

 You know, it took me a while to even notice them.

 It just all works so well together.

 The earrings do work together very well.

 I mean, I feel like, weirdly, this week your fashion journey has become part of my journey as well. Because every day you've come in and I've been like . . . I've always been afraid to wear a hat like that. Now I'm like, "Well, shit, if Ned can pull it off, yeah, why not me?"

 Why not you? Exactly, this is what this is all about. If I can do it, a father of one, husband of one, generally not a "cool" guy, then anyone can do it. Will I do it again, though? That's the real question.

 I don't think you'll do this outfit again.

 Is this how we all feel when Eugene overdresses?

 I actually saw you out of the corner of my eye and I thought Eugene was here.

 I'm getting really nervous about spilling on my outfit.

 Yeah, I don't know how you get a stain out of that.

 I think you just have to shower while wearing it.

 Oh my God, Eugene! He's wearing the exact same thing! He's wearing the exact same thing! Eugene is wearing the same thing! Eugene, Eugene!

 We did not plan this. Who wore it better?

 I love the outfit. I don't believe you in it, but I love it.

 You don't believe me in it?

 This is queer culture, this is a gay man's outfit. Which I love. I'm all about that.

 I'm not allowed to wear it?

 I don't think you should not wear it. It's just, it's very gay. Which I love. I'm all about that gay life. But this is the least believable I've seen you in an outfit. Stepping out of your fashion comfort zones is great. But in the end, it's also identifying where you want to go with your fashion and how it expresses the real Ned. Right? 'Cause fashion is only what you make of it. Style is your personal choice. In conclusion, I love the outfit, but I don't love it as a Ned outfit. Does that make sense?

 Totally. Hey, is my brim larger than your brim?

 It's not the size of the brim, it's the way you wear it.

 I set you up for that.

WHEN ZACH AND I WENT to the football game, we had to walk through USC's campus to get to the stadium. And we got *mobbed*. I've never been recognized more or gotten more compliments. One girl said to me, "Ned, you look like Beyoncé." I felt jazzed. I mean, is this what it feels like to be Eugene? *Is this what it feels like to be Beyoncé?*

I thought this would be one of the worst weeks of my life, but it's turned out pretty great. I feel like I can do anything. 'Cause I've already done *all the things*. People were coming up to me to take selfies and I told them to buy the book! #FeedWes

The only downside was that during the game my hat was blocking the view of some people behind me, so I took it off. And then, just as Ariel warned me, it started to get chilly and my nips chafed. Luckily, Zach had one of my new favorite accessories—a jean jacket—and was happy to lend it to me.

DAY 5

FASHION FEAR: Skirts, man bags, more jewelry

DEGREE OF ANXIETY: Ultimate

OUTFIT:

* Septum piercing (fake, obv.)
* Long white T-shirt (Zara)
* Cross-body bag (Zara)
* Plaid skirt (Zara Women's)
* Black wash denim (Topshop)
* Chelsea boot (Topman)

ON MY LAST DAY of this experiment, me and Roman really kicked it up a notch. And once again, Ariel kinda dug it (is she messing with me?). She said I look like I'm in a Scottish punk rock wedding band. (I am wearing my own tuxedo jacket, by the way.) Even my son Wes loved the outfit but that's probably because he likes anything that's the color green. Fun fact—I'm wearing a chest pack (not a fanny pack!) because, well, this skirt has no pockets. Oh, and I'm sporting a fake nose ring. It hurt to get on and I know it's gonna hurt to get off. Do I need eyeliner? I feel like I need eyeliner.

So, yep, I'm headed to work in a skirt right now.

~ DAY 5 ~

Did you guys notice the septum ring?

 I see the septum ring. Honestly, Ned, it looks like you're trying to prank us into showering you with praise, but you yourself don't like this outfit.

 No, I love it. I'm into it.

 I don't like this look.

 All right.

 What do you like about it?

 I didn't think that I would enjoy wearing a skirt, but when I look at it in the mirror, it's like it's flowy. It feels, like, fashionable.

 Chest bag's cool.

 I like how it incorporates an element from my actual wardrobe with the tuxedo jacket.

 I can't believe I'm saying this, but it feels incomplete for some reason and I can't quite place it. It's like you're so extra right now but then like your top half is kind of normal.

 Well, I actually have a different perspective. I obviously love this because I basically wear skirts all the time, but I kind of feel like I would personally like it without the jacket or the bag. Because the skirt is where I want my eye to go and right now I'm looking so much at the bag and the suit jacket.

 I think the shirt's too long for this, too.

 Can I see it without the bag?

 Nope! Too bad. You guys don't get to pick. I get to pick my outfit and you just have to look at it, so if you want to wear a plaid skirt with a short shirt and no chest bag on your own, be my fucking guest, but I'm going to wear this and you can all go to hell.

Whoa. Whoa.

 Well, this is a big step for me.

 Good job.

 Are you proud of me for telling you guys to fuck off?

 Yeah.

 You know what? I am.

 Yeah. I mean, I think the big thing is you went 100 percent because all of these pieces are out of your comfort zone, so, I mean, in the end, in your daily fashion, you can always incorporate whatever you want. But you took a big leap, and I'm proud of you.

 And you know what? Normally, all of those things that you guys just said would really affect me and make me feel bad, but because I've put myself out there all week, I'm like, "You know what? It doesn't matter what people think. All that matters is what *I* think."

 I mean, that's kind of the whole idea of being fashionable. Do you think I walk around, wearing weird shit, thinking like, "Oh, God. What if people look at me?" You get to that point where you just wear what you want to wear.

 I do think you think that. I think everybody thinks that.

 Yeah. Eugene looks stupid all the time.

 When you start taking more fashion risks, you start caring less about what people think as opposed to staying in the same box.

LOOKS LIKE we all learned something here today.

In the middle of the day, I went to play a few rounds of golf in my outfit. It was a beautiful day. And it just felt right, you know, because of the plaid? Plus, I had a lot more mobility with the skirt. Though I'm not sure if these stylish Chelsea boots are the best choice for the greens. One guy on the course asked me if it was a Scottish thing, like if I was wearing a kilt. When I told him I just wanted to do something different, he was like, "Oh. Cool. I like different." The only issue came when I had to, well, poop. In a skirt.

I'm not gonna say how I did it. But I did it.

Clothes mean nothing until someone lives in them.

—Marc fucking Jacobs

Overall, it was a pretty crazy week. I wore things that I never thought I'd wear. I gained a level of comfort (and experienced a level of discomfort) that I wasn't expecting. There was a lot of introspection. I sometimes think about the reasons I like acting and theater so much. Part of it actually stems from a discomfort in being yourself. When you get dressed in your ordinary clothes, people might criticize you. But when you're onstage or in film, they can criticize your work, but they can't criticize you—it's just a performance! You can wear clothes that are eccentric or extreme and no one thinks it's strange; you're wearing a costume.

One thing I learned throughout this week is that all clothing is a costume. As the week went on, I realized that my "normal" clothes already told a story: as a dad, a husband, and a creator. Every single thing you put onto your body is something that you—either consciously or not—are projecting to the world. Once I realized that, fashion became much more active for me. It wasn't just "What should I wear that will make other people not make fun of me?" It became "What do I want to say about myself today?" And sometimes that voice says, "I don't care what you think! Go to hell!"

All in all, doing some of these things that were outside my comfort zone built up confidence and made me want to try more aggressive fashion choices moving forward. It gave me the sense that I could do anything I wanted. Other people's opinions no longer mattered.

The day after the challenge ended, a friend saw me in my normal, non-Roman-curated clothes and said, "Hey, are you still doing that fashion thing?" Wow, it must have just been my attitude!

That remark stayed with me for the rest of the day.

WHAT WE LEARNED

* You probably already own some great pieces, but they are buried in the back of your closet. Dig 'em out and try 'em on!

* Improve your wardrobe gradually. Get one new thing and then build around that.

* Hang out with your most fashionable friends, and maybe even bribe them to go shopping with you. Their style will rub off on you.

* Don't worry about what other people think about your outfits. Fashion is about you, not them. Other people are probably jealous anyway. At least that's what you should tell yourself.

CHAPTER FOUR

Work

Whyen you watch our videos, you probably notice the clever jokes and slick editing. But you know what's going on behind the scenes? Absolute fucking mayhem. Twenty emails when one would suffice. Lunch breaks at 5 p.m. or, gasp, not at all. The Try Guys may seem like a well-oiled machine but the only thing well oiled is Eugene's hair.

Achieving work-life balance (or school-life balance, for some of you readers) is something that self-help books love to talk about. And we recommend you read them. But what we're going to do is give you an inside look at our "process," how we started working together, and how we will inevitably take each other's lives in a grim murder-suicide fight over YouTube captions.

Everyone says you should work to live, not live to work, but what happens when you love your job and work with your best friends? What happens when you can't get the creative juices flowing and as a result everyone has to stay late and Ned doesn't get to kiss his baby good night? What happens when The Try Guys stop being polite, and start getting real?

What's Wrong with Us

CREATING WEB CONTENT is a relentless and unforgiving job. Don't get me wrong, it's a blessed position to be in: millions of people see your work, it's fun, you call the shots, and, if done correctly, it can be a fruitful and prosperous career. But it never. Fucking. Stops. We pride ourselves on making high-value videos, but that doesn't change the nature of the platform; success on the internet is ephemeral and it's all about a steady stream of content. *What's next?* There's a reason so many Web personalities have come forward with stories of burnout and unyielding stress. Creating videos for the Web means you're constantly vying for flighty attention and competing with every other piece of content that has ever been produced in the history of the world. It's easy to find yourself always feeling like you should be doing more, that any moment wasted is a moment you're losing your competitive edge.

In early 2018 we launched a new company and channel, and with that I eradicated any semblance of work-life balance. When your job is also your hobby, it leaves you with very few other desires in life; everything I want is all in one place. It also means I'm terrible at keeping up with other basic life functions, like seeing friends and, you know, actually taking care of myself.

Lately I've started losing my ability to enjoy my work. As the stresses have mounted, less of my time is spent doing what I love and more of it is spent putting out fires and being reactive. With each additional responsibility, I feel less in control of my own life, and years of neglecting work-life balance have finally caught up to me. For the first time, my job has become *a job.*

MY WORK-LIFE BALANCE has gotten so bad it's reached the point that I can't enjoy my Saturdays without some amount of guilt that I am not working. Even on my anniversary with Becky (we went to Disneyland, the happiest place on earth), I felt terrible about not going into work because there was just so much to do. I checked some emails and tried to do some work; Becky was kind enough to not mention that she noticed until the next day. I can only imagine what it's like for Ned. He has the same amount of work as me, plus he thinks the most about company financials, *plus he has a human baby.*

We have so many goals. They all feel within reach, but our problem is that we are trying to reach them all at once. It's like being at the most delicious buffet and having one plate. You start at one end filling it with all the stuff you like, but then you continue down and there's even better stuff, and you wish you hadn't wasted the space on the first stuff, but you didn't know there was gonna be prime rib at

KEITH'S PROCRASTINATION PROBLEM

My bad habits at work stretch into all aspects of my life. I have this tendency to let things get out of control, and then run away from them and ignore the problem, and then stress out over how out of control everything is and try to fix it all at once. Here's a great example that will resonate with a lot of people and absolutely horrify others.

In case it's not clear, I'm referring to my 6,883 unread emails in the top right. I used to be really good about keeping that number down, but slowly I just lost control and gave up. Now I'm so used to it that it doesn't even bother me. The only messages that get real attention on my phone are texts.

Also, check out the single Facebook Messenger notification I have on the left. I know what it is. It's someone on a group thread who had to bail on an Airbnb because he got sick at the last minute and said he would pay the two hundred dollars anyway. I felt conflicted. On the one hand, yes, he should pay because he committed and that's not our fault. On the other, he's already having a shitty weekend having to miss a wedding, being sick, and having the guilt of owing people money. I didn't know how to respond so *I just didn't*. And I didn't even open it so it wouldn't say that I read it. I just totally ran away from the problem. And now it sits there like Edgar Allan Poe's "The Raven." When will my guilt-induced procrastination stop? Quoth the iPhone: "Nevermore."

A BRIEF HISTORY OF TRYING

- - - - - - - - - -

When the merger of Time Warner and AOL was announced in 2000, it was hailed as a visionary combination of the old economy and the new that would leave all other internet and content companies in the dust. Just two years later, the combined megafirm had to take a $99 billion—that's *billion* with a *b*—write-off and the whole thing is now considered the worst merger of all time. There's no silver lining here, just a reminder that even smart people do really dumb shit.

the end. I can only equate stress to food. Or maybe it's just because I'm still vegan right now and I secretly want nothing more than to stuff my face.

THROUGH MOST OF MY TWENTIES, I felt like I had a pretty solid work-life balance. I was good at organizing tasks, setting long-term goals, and carving out personal time to travel the world and have weekly date nights. I brought my lunch pail to work every day, cranked out viral hits, then left. But that all changed when I had a baby. So far, it seems *impossible* to have work-life balance with a newborn. There are not enough hours in the day. I wake up at 6 a.m., yet so much of the morning is spent caring for the baby that often I'm not able to actually start working until 10 a.m. But I treasure my mornings with Wes, so it's all a tough balancing act. The other guys have been very supportive of me needing to take time off or leave early, but the guilt of not working eats away at me. It makes me worried that I'm not doing enough. In this chapter I'm hoping to learn some better time-management skills and communication strategies so that I can fully unplug and be present with my family. I want to work hard and play hard.

WHAT THE HELL does work-life balance mean, anyway? Life, for me, is what happens around and after your most pressing work projects. Even when I try to go on a rare vacation—like I did last year for New Year's in Hawaii—I treat it like work, creating a tourism schedule that typically requires a 6 a.m. wake-up, overflowing with activities and monuments and ending sometime after midnight. Without question, my "life" is and has always been my "work."

For many in creative fields, the line between what constitutes work and play is extremely blurry. Much of my balance, then, is influenced by the love I feel toward what I'm working on. If I'm inspired by a video or script or role I'm pursuing, then work begins to feel a lot more like living life to the fullest. Now, as green, first-time business owners, The Try Guys don't always have the luxury to solely work on artistic fulfillment—in fact, most of what has populated our calendars lately has been managerial, financial, and administrative in nature. We crucially need a comprehensive mental makeover in order to get four poetic boys to transform into responsible businessmen.

Portrait of the Artist as a Young Man

THE RUTHLESS EDUCATION and employment culture in East Asia is no joke. I probably would have grown up to be a hard-drinking salaryman had I not dodged a bullet by displaying some wunderkind abilities as a young artist. I drew better than all my peers. My art projects were shown off to the entire school. I aced every music memory exam. I was gifted with the rare opportunity as a child to show my parents that if I were to pursue a creative field, I could be the best at it. Lord knows that if I had finger-painted a medio-cre dinosaur in kindergarten, my folks sure as hell would've pushed math and science on me harder. I was gifted with an innate knack for performance and an ironclad work ethic to prove that their support of my passions would not be in vain. I was in one season of basketball, and was painfully aware of how unskilled I was compared to the bigger kids. My dad pulled me aside and said, "Quitting something you're bad at only makes you less of a waste of time, so don't be ashamed."

After graduating from USC film school—arguably the

top cinema education program in the world—my head held high, inflated by the countless successes I had as a student, I fell face-first into a depressed economy. To support myself as I worked toward my ultimate career goals, I supplemented freelance projects with several years of what most every young artist turns to: waiting tables.

Dim sum, to be exact. I shuttled bamboo steamer after bamboo steamer filled with juicy pork dumplings to an upscale Westside crowd who said things like, "Does this have MSG?" "I can't eat anything that was breathing." "Do you have regular Chinese food?" I wanted to roast my brains alongside the ducks after every shift, but I maintained a chipper demeanor and constant, sharklike focus because I knew, at the end of the day, that I had to support myself. Besides my basic needs, I was also supporting my art, and when I wasn't at the restaurant, I was directing and editing music videos and commercials and participating in whatever film developmental programs I could find.

So even though I despised putting on my apron and considered my service position an abject failure when compared to the dreams I had sketched out about where I'd be by my mid-twenties (helming huge Hollywood productions), I realized that it was only a failure if I treated it as such, and so I approached my job waiting tables with the same gusto and commitment that I had when I picked up a camera. I met countless connections and wonderful collaborators during my time cleaning up dishes—people with whom I still work to this day.

Unfortunately, life is not always a smoothly paved road, and although we will discuss the troubles of being new business owners in this chapter, it's a vaunted position we all worked extremely hard to achieve. My path happened to be littered with empty dumpling baskets and countless nights directing projects I should've been paid far more for. In this five-year freelance period of obscurity, toil, shitty gigs, and explaining to non-Asians what *shu mai* is, my creative output was robust but my salary was nonexistent. I was living off pennies and had to schedule the times when I would beg my parents to send money to help me stay afloat. Even though I worked my ass off, this could've been the time that my father pulled me aside and said, "You know, son, maybe this whole entertainment thing isn't working. Maybe you should hang up your jersey and find a different sport."

But I never stopped trying, and fascinatingly enough, my foray into the digital industry was completely by happenstance. I had zero interest in working for BuzzFeed, but I had even less enthusiasm about paying rent with my nightly tips, and so I wandered into the brand-new video branch of an internet start-up with slumped shoulders, believing that at my age and with my pedigree of education, to accept an internship there would be the final nail in my coffin of failed aspirations. The bottom line was that I needed a full-time job, and at the very least this office felt new, confusing, and exciting, and so I accepted the offer with few plans to stay there beyond a few months.

Just like my art projects in grade school and my shifts as a server, I decided that there was no benefit in treating my new role as if I had failed (even though I thought I had), and so I undertook the experience with unbridled dedication and an open mind. I ended up working there for more than four years—the longest steady job I ever had—and the rest is viral history. I turned what I could have viewed as total crap into career gold, and it took years of training myself to approach my studies, my jobs, and my dreams with the defiantly confident mind-set that I would get something valuable out of anything I put my soul into. In doing so, all of my potential failures were spun into relative successes because I never, ever stopped trying.

> One day, in retrospect, the years of struggle will strike you as the most beautiful.
>
> —*Sigmund fucking Freud*

Jacksonville to Yale

MY HIGH SCHOOL in Florida put on several theater productions every year, including a night of student-written and student-produced one-acts, which is how I first got involved in performing. It was really fun entertaining an audience, but I never really knew how to make a career out of it, so, since I was also in my high school's robotics club, I went to college thinking that I wanted to be an engineer or a scientist. Although I got into a few engineering schools (I even got a robotics scholarship to USC—Eugene and I could have been roomies!), they seemed restrictive in that their coursework was *only* math and science. Instead I chose the liberal arts route and attended Yale University.

The day I got my admissions letter I ran all around the house jumping up and down. The other guys make fun of Yale, but it really was an amazing experience: world-class professors, lifelong friendships, and—most important—an entrepreneurial theater and film scene. There were a wide variety of opportunities to apply for grants of a few thousand dollars to create new productions. That, plus the connection to the renowned Yale School of Drama, made it a buzzing hub where there were dozens of theater productions and film projects created by students every semester. I got involved with an improv group called The Purple Crayon, named after the children's book. I acted Shakespeare, I wrote scripts, I did stand-up, and by the end of college I had even written and produced two episodes of a twenty-two-minute original sitcom. You didn't need to wait for a gatekeeper to cast you in something or give you permission to do something. You could find friends and produce it yourself.

But I still didn't know how to make a career out of it, so I continued studying science and math, which I loved. Don't disrespect math, y'all. Math makes the world go round.

The summer after freshman year, I worked in a basement laser spectroscopy lab, resuscitating an old time-of-flight mass spectrometer to look at argon nano-matrix clusters. OMG, what did I just write? I'm supposed to be a YouTuber now. (Clears throat.) These views are lit AF. (Dabs violently.) Anyway, since doing research in a dark basement all summer was actually really fun, I decided to major in chemistry. I figured you could do comedy with a chemistry degree but you couldn't do chemistry with a comedy degree. However, over time, I found the amount of writing and performing I did increased, and the amount of time I spent studying decreased. I would stay up all night editing a comedy video and barely make it to my actual p-chem (physical chemistry) class the next day.

After college, my first chemistry job in Chicago (while I was performing at night) was working in a group called the Rapid Analytical Testing Service, or RATS, at the Stepan Company. We were the analytical testing arm of a research division for a major surfactant manufacturer. "Surfactant" is a fancy word for soap. So I was the guy making sure your shampoo was foamy enough and your dish soap actually cleaned your pots. True story.

It's a fun anecdote to tell at parties, but as a job it was impossibly boring. Little vials of liquid would get dropped off in my lab through a slot. They would have a number printed on them. I would look up the number in the computer. I would take the little vial of liquid and run the assigned test on it, following the procedure. The tests would take anywhere from twenty minutes to two hours. Then I would type the results into the computer and dispose of the vial. Little squirts of soap go in. Numbers go out.

Steve Jobs was fired from Apple, the company he founded, in 1985. But he bided his time and returned to the company in 1997, became a bajillionaire, and now you're reading this on an iPad on the toilet.

Having no connection to the thought process behind why we were running tests was tough. I liked studying science because it was interesting and challenging. But this job was flipping burgers with chemicals. I tried to actively be bad at my day job, leaving early to go to rehearsals and writing scripts while my experiments were running. I got very familiar with the alt + tab keyboard shortcut to flip from a script to a spreadsheet whenever anyone walked behind me. I knew that I ultimately wanted a creative career where I had a high degree of autonomy and control over my own work. I wanted to know why I was doing things.

I worked there for less than two months.

The Path Less Traveled

THERE'S NO WAY to know what path your career will take. After college, I moved out to Los Angeles with a film production degree and some incredibly lofty goals. I'd charted out my career pretty meticulously: direct music videos for my favorite LA bands, get hired to make sketches at Funny or Die (the *only* internet company worth my time), land a high-powered agent, dominate the festival circuit, then beat away studios with a stick as they all desperately bid on my next film. My professional reality . . . did not follow that plan. Not even fucking close.

The next year was a steady humbling of my dreams. I spent months cold-emailing bands, nervously approaching musicians after shows, and just trying to get my treatments in front of anyone who would read them. Nobody responded; I was just some kid without a meaningful credit to my name. I thought about financing something myself but, oh yeah, I was broke. I interviewed for a director's assistant position at Funny or Die and never heard back. I finally landed a job at one of the coolest production companies in town . . . as an unpaid intern doing script coverage (that's where you read screenplays and tell your boss why they shouldn't make them—Hollywood hates risk). With my savings drying up fast, it was time to rethink the master plan.

The next two years was a menagerie of unexpected turns and saying yes to opportunities as they came my way. I followed up with an old internship contact, and she recommended me to a producer in need of eager, cheap labor. I fell into the PA (production assistant) circuit, working on commercial shoots, and suddenly I was on *actual* sets with a front-row seat to watch the biggest directors in the world do their thing. I worked my ass off, the producers took notice, and soon I found myself in the coveted office PA role. I now joined productions not just on set, but also accompanying the team for all of preproduction, auditions, location scouts, and more. After two years, I'd established myself as a mainstay of the team and seldom had more than a few days between freelance gigs. It was an incredible education, and one I actually got paid for.

Random connections continued to pave the road forward. Through a PA friend, I found myself volunteering at a weekly comedy show—a much-needed anchor for someone with a totally irregular schedule. There I got free admission to watch some of the world's most prominent and rising comedians workshop their acts. When they found out I was a director, it was the in I needed to start filming sketches again, this time with talent beyond my wildest imagination. One of these connections birthed a Web series called *The Fresh Manager of Jaden Smith* (yes, that's the real title and we nailed it). Through making *that* I met Ella Mielniczenko, who would go on to become a best friend but for this story is most notable for being the first person to tell me about BuzzFeed. I politely told her that while I only had a passing knowledge of BuzzFeed, it was enough to know I did not want to work there. But after months of chipping away, she finally convinced me to join her on the team. After the first week, it was very clear that it was a special place to be.

Someway, somehow, years of random connections and "not achieving my dreams" led me down a path of success. You couldn't plan it if you tried. Life is chaotic and random, and the only thing you can do is work hard and remain open to opportunities as they come your way. I didn't achieve my dreams, and that's okay, because the real thing has been so much better.

Candyman

MY FIRST JOB was in middle school when, ahem, I ran my very own business! It actually came out of a school project. In seventh-grade science class, we had to create an edible chemistry experiment (kinda weird, I know) and I chose making "sugar glass." It's breakaway glass like they use in movies when a character gets thrown through a window, but it's literally made of sugar! I made the glass, but I didn't cook it long enough, I guess, because when I broke it over my head (natch), it didn't shatter as much as I'd hoped. Instead it broke off into big thick chunks. One of the kids in class picked it up and put it in his mouth—classic middle school move—and said it was totally awesome. Other kids picked up the pieces and ate them, and some kid said, "I'd pay for this!" *Lightbulb!*

The next weekend I tried making it in an ice cube tray, but it came out superchewy. So I made another batch, and another, until I figured out how to make the right consistency. I took some pieces to school for my friends, and some kids paid me a whole dollar for an ice-cube-sized piece. Cut to a week later and I had developed eight different flavors, scaled down the sizes of my pieces, started charging a quarter per piece, and was bringing in $150 gross revenue each week. Eventually the school caught on and told me I couldn't do that anymore. But I was not deterred. . . .

"What if it's a fund-raiser for the school's book program?" I asked.

They didn't know how much I was making, so I told them I made about $50 a week, minus expenses. So each week I gave them about $40 and I pocketed $100. I guess I was kinda like a kid mafia. I paid off the government (school) to let me sell my goods (candy). It was pretty sweet—pun intended— and I did it for the last couple of months of the school year. At the end-of-year awards ceremony, I was even given a trophy for my fund-raising. It said: "For outstanding dedication to the school—Keith 'The Candyman' Habersberger."

I've always loved making things. From little weird projects in my backyard, to goofy improvised productions at college, to viral videos. Making things that bring people joy, from comedy to candy, has always been my calling. And if can I skim a little bit off the top from a junior high school's book program . . . even better.

2nd Try

WHEN WE FORMED our own company, 2nd Try LLC, we officially became bosses. Sorry, I just vomited a little in my mouth. Now we weren't just creative weirdos, we were *businessmen*, and our every decision affected both our own ability to eat as well as the livelihood of our employees. We found ourselves having to think about things like infrastructure, payroll, scheduling, managing . . .

if there's a problem with our company health insurance, *people will literally die*. It came with a ton of unforeseen challenges, and as we rocketed toward launch, the four of us divvied up tasks in an effort to accomplish the maddening amount of work before us.

I found myself having to learn new skills and rise to challenges unrelated to the creative aspects of my job: managing careers, learning to delegate, and creating the educational infrastructure that our staff operates and grows from. Not to mention the more mechanical decisions like "What equipment should we buy," which was a whole to-do. I'm used to doing everything myself, which is obviously not sustainable, nor is it scalable. The four of us are total control freaks and perfectionists, but those traits don't lend themselves well to efficiency. In starting this company we knew we wanted to expand into new arenas and that meant bringing others into the flow of our work. But managing others hasn't been my biggest struggle; it's been learning to manage my own time.

RUNNING OUR OWN COMPANY has been our greatest challenge. We are now our own bosses and we don't know how to stop working. That's the bottom line, and we know that many CEOs suffer similarly packed schedules with little to no room for everyday life to seep through. Reacquainting ourselves with one another as leaders of a self-run business has been a fascinating flexing of our singular strengths: for example, while Ned handles budgeting and spreadsheets, I've picked up more responsibility for creative pitches and branding.

WHEN WE WERE MAKING PLANS to leave BuzzFeed, we were confident we could get views on our own and were excited about creating a deeper fan community, but how did that translate to an actual business model? Our first few months were just going to be spending lots of our own real, actual money in a hopeful expectation of future, predicted money that my spreadsheets said we would theoretically make. It was daunting! Would I be able to feed Wes? As the most finance-savvy member of The Try Guys, that was my job to figure out.

Early on, I developed a business model for what Try Guys 2.0 would look like as an independent company. I projected how much money we could expect to

EXPERT ADVICE FROM KEVIN LIN

KEVIN is the cofounder of video game streaming site Twitch, which was acquired by Amazon for a cool $1 billion in 2014. He's a tech investor, video game aficionado, and dude who knows how to get shit done.

Here are his tips for having a more productive workday:

✳ Use the Wunderlist app to organize your tasks and to-do lists, the Pocket app to save articles to read later, and an Oura Ring activity tracker to track sleep and combat jet lag.

✳ Wear the same thing every day—one less thing to think about. I wear jeans and a black Mack Weldon T-shirt. I have twenty of them! And if you can't wear the same thing every day, at least pick out your outfit the night before, so you're not wasting crucial seconds (and neurons) getting ready for work in the morning.

✳ Block off time when no one can bother you. At Twitch, if you see someone wearing noise-canceling headphones, that means "Please do not disturb."

✳ Procrastination is necessary! Seriously. Your brain and body need to rest. I may be biased, but I recommend video games.

bring in from YouTube versus sponsorships versus other projects, like this book or our merch line or even a potential TV show. I estimated our costs: how much money (and time) we each would personally need to invest and how many people we should hire to help us. At one point I calculated that the only way we could accomplish all of our goals was if there were eighteen months in a year. Whoops. We had to prioritize. It was a lot of responsibility and I am honored to have earned the trust of the other Try Guys. I am incredibly protective of them and of our business. They're my family.

THROWBACK: Look at these confused lil entrepreneurs in training.

IN THE EARLY MONTHS of the company, with Ned's baby arriving early and Eugene being out of state for a project, some early responsibilities fell on Zach and myself. We were pretty daunted, but there was really no way around it. Personally, I was scared and overwhelmed. I really don't excel at business stuff, but there we were sitting at the bank trying to figure out what we needed to do to open a business account and get ourselves approved by the state of California. I was in email chains with different video and audio libraries trying to find out what was affordable and would serve our company's needs. We were doing interviews, hiring PAs, and scheduling the shoots and releases for when everybody was back. It was wild. At some point I found myself creating all the banner assets for all our social media pages. I am probably one of the weaker Photoshop artists of the group, but there wasn't enough manpower to go around, so I just learned how to be better.

Probably the biggest contribution I made to the company in the first months was setting up our Patreon. It's a platform for our biggest fans to subscribe to premium content from us at different price tiers. It was a ton of work, and something we almost didn't do, but thank God we did, because it ended up being one of the most essential and rewarding parts of

our business. YouTube pays out its revenue one month after it's earned, so with our channel launching mid-June and a two-week delay to even get approved for monetization, the first real check we would get would be at the end of August. We had already been paying staff out of our own pockets since April, so we were quickly running out of money. Patreon was the *only* revenue we had coming in at the time. We are so appreciative of our Tryceratops (what we call our patrons) because we literally couldn't have done it without them. We learned that you don't always know which part of your business will be most valuable, so sometimes you have to take a chance on the opportunities that come your way, no matter how uncertain they may be. Also, we really need to manage our time better or we're never gonna make it. . . .

Only those who dare to fail greatly can ever achieve greatly.

—*Robert F. Kennedy*
(the F stands for Fucking)

The Try Guys Try to Work like CEOs!

For this try, we talked to experts like Oprah Winfrey, Mark Zuckerberg, and Richard Branson. Okay we googled them, compiled all their best practices into a spreadsheet (thanks, Ned), and put together the ultimate, totally optimized, play-like-a-champion CEO workday, hour by hour. Each of us is going to try to follow this regimen for a day and see if it kicks us into high gear—or drives us directly into the ground.

MORNING

5:00 A.M.   Wake up and . . . meditate. (WTF?)

5:30 A.M.   Exercise. Yes, even though it's still dark outside.

6:30 A.M.   Make your bed. Generals do it.

6:45 A.M.   Write in a journal—things you're grateful for, things you can improve on, and what your intentions are for the day.

7:00 A.M.   Breakfast: Just coffee.

7:30 A.M.   Read news headlines and social media (aka, just read social media).

8:00 A.M.   Shower and put on your daily uniform (that is, the same outfit you wear every day).

9:30 A.M.   Take a series of meetings back-to-back in one long block, usually not longer than seven minutes each. Always have a notebook on hand to write down ideas.

AFTERNOON

12:00 P.M. Lunch—finally!

1:00 P.M. "Think time" (task-free time to think about the "bigger picture").

1:40 P.M. Do brief face-to-face check-ins with your team. (Also, no more caffeine from here on out; sorry.)

2:30 P.M. Dedicated three-hour work block divided up with "timeboxing"— allotting a fixed, maximum unit of time for a preplanned activity, the way God intended it.

5:30 P.M. Group dinner.

7:45 P.M. Go home.

NIGHT

8:30 P.M. "Escort" electronic devices out of your room.

9:00 P.M. Unwind by doing chores. Or taking a walk outside without music.

9:30 P.M. Take a hot bath with Epsom salts.

10:00 P.M. Change into clothes dedicated specifically to sleep and nothing else.

10:15 P.M. Drink chamomile or lavender tea.

10:30 P.M. Write down the things that you're grateful for today.

10:45 P.M. Go to sleep.

5:00 A.M.

Wake up and . . . meditate. (WTF?)

I WOKE UP at 4:30 a.m. so I'm already ahead! But I did not meditate and instead drank coffee in bed.

HA-HA-HA. YEAH RIGHT. Sleep is a precious commodity for a new dad. No way I'm waking up at 5:00 a.m. just to meditate; 1:00 a.m.—Wake up and feed the baby; 4:00 a.m.—Wake up and feed the baby; 6:00 a.m.—Wake up. Start meditating. Get five minutes in when the baby cries and interrupts me.

NOT A CHANCE am I waking up that early. It's still dark out! On a good day I wake up somewhere in the 7:00–8:30 a.m. range depending on how late I was up the night before. Usually I'll scroll through Twitter and check my other apps with one eye open until my fourth alarm goes off and I reluctantly roll out of bed. For this experiment I decided to set my alarm for 6:00 a.m. as a fair compromise.

SLEEP IS A LUXURY I have yet to learn how to maximize, but I make it a major priority to get a decent seven to eight hours. I usually prefer evening over morning workouts since my compulsions keep me up, with lights-out around 2:00 a.m. on average and rising around 8:00 a.m. I also occasionally suffer from bouts of insomnia, more often when there are pressing work engagements that occupy my focus. Long story short, if snoozing were a class subject, I would have gotten an F.

To get the proper amount of sleep and be up at 5:00 a.m. would mean being in bed by 10:00 p.m., which actually made me laugh out loud. A 10:00 p.m. lights-out made me feel like some unruly toddler who's required to go night-night. I lay there, eyes trained on the ceiling fan, fighting off all temptation to glance at my phone, knowing its blue incandescence would make it an even steeper uphill battle to close my eyes.

5:30 A.M.

Exercise. Yes, even though it's still dark outside.

 I TOOK a 6:00 a.m. class at Orangetheory and am feeling pretty darn good about it, thank you very much. I'm still working out from chapter 2!

 NO TIME FOR THIS because I "slept in" all the way to 6:00 a.m. I will instead do "baby squats," where I do squats while holding Wes. He has a great time flying through the air and I add 18.5 pounds to my workout.

 STILL SLEEPING.

 AS I ELABORATED upon in the health chapter, I crave exercise like a drug and go into severe withdrawal when I can't get my heart rate up. Walking into a circuit class this morning, then, was like taking a strong hit of something I'm addicted to, and I immediately felt my entire mood lighten.

It's upper body day at Training Mate, a boutique studio that is walking distance from my apartment and a personal favorite of mine because the trainers are all extremely attractive Australian models who yell at you in sexy accents with dirty jokes that would be an HR violation in any other setting, such as: "Reach down and grab the balls, but don't tug them too hard!" "Squat for some hot buns like you did last Saturday night!" and "Yank the rower like you're back in grade school discovering yourself for the first time!"

After the final round of abs, I leave with the exhilarating, almost peaceful sense of accomplishment you feel only after completing a very early morning class. As the sun peeks over the tree line, it dawns on me that, with my head surprisingly serene and uncluttered, the exercise worked in lieu of my miserable meditation attempt. I made the mental note that, if anything, changing to a.m. exercises might supercharge my day.

6:30 A.M.
Make your bed. Generals do it.

 I DID NOT make my bed. There is no time for that and also who cares.

 OKAY, now we're back on track. Yes, I love making my bed. It feels like I accomplished something already today. I'm a goddamn CEO now.

 ALAS, ya boi is awake! I can't make the bed because my girlfriend Maggie is still in it, so I'm calling that one a freebie. Also, I hate making my bed. I'm not about to make my sheets all neat just to mess it up again tonight. Eventually I decide to fold my side of the covers and prop one pillow up. I did something.

 THIS SUGGESTION—to make my bed—struck me as particularly counterproductive, since it's always been my lazy male philosophy that a permanently unmade bed is the natural state. My opinions on the merits of tidiness expose one of my greatest flaws as a contributing member of the human race: outside of creative projects, I'm a totally disorganized, clutter-loving mess.

But I perform the ritual, begrudgingly, and discover a never-before-seen, suspicious yellow spot—which I would eventually determine to be one of my dogs' vomit—was drying on my covers for God knows how long. So if anything, making your bed like a CEO aids in lessening your chances of sleeping in puppy puke.

6:45 A.M.
Write in a journal—things you're grateful for, things you can improve on, and what your intentions are for the day.

 NOPE. I'm already writing this fucking book. Also, it takes fifteen minutes to make your bed?

I'M ON BABY DUTY in the mornings so journaling was a little tricky. I couldn't really write anything down but I told Wes some things I was grateful for—like our peaceful mornings together and a loving, supportive spouse and having three best friends to start a company with—which was a nice, positive start to my mental day.

I START every morning by walking Bowie for twenty to thirty minutes, which is sort of like meditation, and then I do about twenty minutes of stretching exercises targeting my AS. Since I'm running behind I decided to skip the journal thing, though I admit, in all of this, that piece sounds the loveliest. I think I'll try it moving forward. During my walk I set the day's intentions to make the most of my time and to—please, God—just fucking make it through the day.

I HAVE NOT and will never write in a journal. It has always made me slightly uncomfortable knowing that my innermost thoughts could be accessible in a tangible location. Surely that could be used as a form of blackmail someday, as I've been taught by every eighties movie starring vindictive teenage girls. Since I trust my computer's hard drive as a theoretically safer space to store my thoughts, I decide to make a journal entry digitally:

THINGS I AM GRATEFUL FOR

* I'm grateful that our burgeoning company has proven to be a wise and marginally profitable venture.
* I'm grateful that my passions and my career directly align.
* I'm grateful that I still have all my amazing hair.

THINGS I CAN IMPROVE ON

* I can improve on being more open and vulnerable, and admit my weaknesses with my loved ones, especially the other Try Guys for the sake of our business.
* I can improve on my overall hair care regimen.

MY INTENTIONS FOR TODAY

* Live my day like a true boss and hopefully learn how to maximize my efficiency and productivity.
* Stick to the plan with an open mind, even when history and personal bias threaten it.
* Make my hair look good.

7:00 A.M.
Breakfast: Just coffee.

 JUST COFFEE? I have a feeling this is gonna be a tough one for the gang to follow. I had a greens smoothie, but it was at 7:30 so I'm already behind and feeling stressed.

I ATE CEREAL while I fed Wes oatmeal. I did try Bulletproof coffee, though (coffee with butter in it). Huge mistake. Putting a tablespoon of butter in my coffee ruined it. I love the ritual of making and drinking coffee in the morning. It helps me wake up and focus on my day. I also like the way it tastes at the end. This tasted exactly how it sounds: *buttery*.

 I'VE GOT a sensitive Jew tummy so I stuck with my daily morning smoothie and tea.

A HUGE HEALTH NO-NO I've been trying to combat is my terrible meal habits. I've steadfastly trained my body since college to only require an enormous dinner and coffee to stave off hunger at all other times of the day. No snacking. No breakfast. No lunch. Just supper and caffeine. I call it "the hyperwarrior's diet."

Today, though, I did my best impression of the other guys, who, like most organisms with a digestive tract, enjoy their morning breakfasts and become increasingly "hangry" when unfed. I had two cups of coffee, a banana, boiled a couple of eggs, and decided to try to whip together the prototypical millennial brunch item—avocado toast. This schedule calls for *no* coffee in the second half of the day, and I begin to dread what is to come.

7:30 A.M.
Read news headlines and social media
(aka, just read social media).

 I LOOKED at my phone while on the toilet and then showered. TMI?

 NEWS??? DONE. EASY. NO PROBLEM. ANXIETY LEVEL INCREASED. (Also: where is "check fantasy football scores" on this schedule?)

WAY AHEAD OF YOU. I already did that in bed, periodically during Bowie's walk, while brushing my teeth, and while peeing. But I'm addicted to my phone so I don't mind spending a little extra time refreshing my apps aimlessly. I used this time to peek at my emails, too. Usually I mark emails as unread as a sort of reminder and to-do list, but since I'm good at ignoring things right in front of me I'm able to let them sit there for weeks if not months. This time was good to finally tackle one of those unanswered emails from a friend who must've thought I was dead by now.

HERE'S ONE THING I know I'm more adroit at than the other guys. I can find ways to keep myself from constantly checking the news and social media. I'm sure that the addiction to our phones contributes massively to negating solid work and study output, and I'm positive that half an hour would be far too long a block dedicated to scrolling through my feeds . . . until I take a gander at the time after what feels like five minutes. I had actually gone slightly overtime, lost in what was clearly a tear in the time-space continuum, and am fascinated by how totally absorbed I became with my Instagram and trending topics, clicking through them with the captivated precision of a robot on an assembly line. I push my phone away, turning it facedown on my table, suddenly more mindful of its eerie, Matrix-like hold over my attention.

8:00 A.M.
Shower and put on your daily uniform
(that is, the same outfit you wear every day).

 I DON'T WEAR the same thing every day but I also didn't waste any energy thinking about what to wear because I truly don't care.

FINALLY! I've gotten so stressed out trying new clothing for the fashion chapter that I forgot how comforting it can be to not think about what I'm wearing. Today I'm rocking our Tryceratops Squad T-shirt with jeans and boots.

THIS BOY IS SHOWERED, clean, and looking hawt in his turtleneck! For my day as CEO I opted to wear a black turtleneck and loose blue jeans. I assume adopting this outfit is the only thing separating me from being Steve Jobs. That, and a proclivity for soaking his feet in toilets (Google it! Or better yet, ask Siri). Being on camera has forced me to spend a ton of time every morning thinking about how I look, and it's refreshing to be fully dressed in five minutes without an ounce of care.

TO THIS PHILOSOPHY'S CREDIT, I do devote a considerable amount of decision-making energy toward what I'm going to wear each morning. So in order to conserve precious neurons and reach peak productivity today, I slipped into the same look I had on yesterday: black jeans, gray Chelsea boots, a sweater, and a wide-brimmed hat. This was probably the most traumatic experience of the day.

9:30 A.M.

Take a series of meetings back-to-back in one long block, usually not longer than seven minutes each. Always have a notebook on hand to write down ideas.

I HAD A DISCUSSION with the guys about how we are organizing our time, which ironically wasted an hour. I tried to get some editing done. I handled an avalanche of emails about a million random topics in no particular order.

THIS WAS MY FAVORITE PART of the day. I crushed these meetings. Having the time pressure of seven minutes really forced me to be efficient. I met with our production manager Alexandria for seven minutes to talk about the budget for an upcoming project, then with our PA Kasiemobi for seven minutes to get an update on bonus content she was making for our Patreon, then with our editor Devlin for seven minutes to discuss a rough cut, and then with Zach for seven minutes to trash-talk his fantasy football team.

NOW, this is where things got tricky. Normally our meetings last thirty minutes, if not an hour. A lot of our meetings are creative problem-solving and brainstorms, and you need that time to make breakthroughs and think through problems. Plus, we all just like to chat a bunch, so that holds us back. At Kevin Lin's suggestion, I purchased noise-canceling headphones and made it known that I could only be reached via slack and appointment for the day instead of having people just come up and tap on my shoulder. It was time to buckle up—seven minutes is not a lot of time and I had a ton that needed to get done.

First, I spent seven minutes firing off emails as fast as my fingers could type. Normally I reread my emails to make sure my syntax is correct and that I'm saying things in an intelligent and tactful way. Today I stuck with shorthand and managed to crush five and a half emails. On a normal day I'd be checking my email several times an hour, more as a procrastination technique, but today I knew I wouldn't be checking it again until right before lunch.

Next I checked in with our producer about a project I'm in charge of, then touched base with the group about the podcast we're testing since I'm the creative lead. About twenty-one minutes in and I was feeling like a goddamn stud. Seven minutes wasn't enough to make a video thumbnail but at least I'd come up with a plan for how to attack it later.

Then I met with one of our editors and that's where things went off the rails. Seven minutes turned into twenty-four minutes as we discussed options and I answered questions. Our videos are sometimes twenty minutes long and there was just too much to talk about. From this point forward, all my seven-minute increments started to bleed into longer chunks of time. Back in our office the guys were debating the best way to structure a video and since I'm the smartest and best they obviously needed my input. That ate up thirteen minutes. Then Ned sent us all the new Dude Perfect video (he loves those guys), and watching YouTube is basically research, so that felt like ten minutes well spent. We had a conference call scheduled for a potential branded video, and as much as I wanted to hang up on the client after seven minutes, I was stuck on there for *forty-two* minutes.

Even though I fell short of my goals, it was by far the most productive morning I'd ever had. I'm typically a slow starter and spend most of my morning putzing around, not making much progress until after lunch. Breaking my morning into strict time units lit a major fire under my ass. My buns were appropriately toasty and ready to roll into the afternoon.

I ARRIVED at the office and immediately beelined for the coffee drip, craving one more hit. And then one more. What normally would happen from here on out is totally dependent on whatever was scheduled: video shoots, business meetings, staff check-ins, editing notes, out-of-office appointments—every day is a grab bag of possibilities. Today I determined that there are several pressing items I need to work on. I knocked out all my calls and emails, while alerting our staff that I'd be enforcing a closed-door policy in the morning, moving my face-to-face time with them to after lunch.

Keith reminds us that he has a deadline for a video edit and promptly plugs in his headphones to drown us out. The black hole of editing for any creative in the filmmaking field is dark and full of terrors, and I know that he will not be able to return from its grasp anytime soon. Keith is lost to us.

12:00 P.M.
Lunch–finally!

SUGGESTIONS

✳ Salad, turkey burger, and sweet potato—Mark Wahlberg

✳ Cheeseburger—Bill Gates

✳ Oatmeal raisin bars—Anderson Cooper

✳ Hamburger without the bun—Anna Wintour

I BROUGHT some boring vegetable dish because I'm vegan now. I don't want to talk about it.

I HAD a cheeseburger for lunch, but I made sure to have it delivered so that I could maximize my productivity. The fries got soggy and eating a cheesy meat sandwich made me feel pretty lethargic. Curious choice, *Bill Gates*.

I'M NOT SURE why Mark Wahlberg's lunch is listed as an example in our CEO schedule. For starters, the obvious must be stated that he's not my go-to image of a CEO. Successful at turning a shtick into a lucrative career, sure. But CEO? Plus, I feel that society just way too easily forgot and forgave the fact that he committed some heinous hate crimes in the 1980s before becoming famous. But damn, his lunch of a turkey burger, salad, and sweet potato sounded both delicious and nutritious, so I decided to go with Marky Mark on this one.

AN HOUR FOR LUNCH always feels like too much time to step away from pressing responsibilities, so I decide to take a stroll a couple of blocks away to a nearby café, rationalizing that the hike, waiting in line, and coming back with the food would eat up some of that countdown. Inadvertently I stumbled upon the rejuvenation of stepping outside into actual sunlight and was almost disheartened by the reminder of how much of the day we spend locked inside, staring at a tiny screen, our postures disintegrating into curved-neck oblivion. My

Mark Wahlberg–inspired fare included a chicken salad sandwich, side salad, and a cup of lentil soup. The same Mark Wahlberg who, when he was young and awful, punched an unsuspecting Asian man in the face for no reason and blinded him. I start to google it before reminding myself that I shouldn't be looking at news or social media if it isn't absolutely necessary.

1:00 P.M.
"Think time"
(task-free time to think about the "bigger picture").

 WHAT KIND OF LIFE is this CEO leading? I have shit to do, and everything I do is part of the bigger picture!

 FOR MY THINK TIME, I walked around the block and thought about the best ways to expand our company and where I wanted The Try Guys to be in five to ten years. Some of my thoughts were about how to grow our ambitions beyond YouTube. Maybe with additional people helping us out we could focus on even bigger things, like new merch collabs or a show on Netflix. Could we create a subscription box that gave people new things to try each month? What about a Try Guys lip kit? Could we take our "Without a Recipe" format to TV? How do I get on the phone with Gordon Ramsay? How do Ariel and I become one of those funny HGTV couples that renovate beautiful houses? Would Chip and Joanna Gaines want to come over and play Settlers of Catan on a double date sometime? Should I try to audition for sitcom roles, or is what I'm doing now

both more fun and more valuable? How *did* Chris Pratt get so shredded? Maybe 2nd Try should just *make our own* sitcoms? Maybe 2nd Try should just *make our own Jurassic Park*?

THIS WAS MY FAVORITE part of the day. My overproductive morning left me way ahead of schedule and I was free to explore my mind palace instead of being bogged down in minutiae. Since I always feel reactive during my workday, I seldom get chances to give mental energy to the big-picture projects.

What really excites me is making shows. I'm always jotting down little ideas but never have a moment to explore them since more pressing deadlines always take precedence. Today I was finally able to return to a long-gestating scripted idea, and episode synopses poured out from me. At the end of the hour I had a full mini-season of episodes charted out and committed to paper. It was there all along, I just needed to dedicate the time to it.

TO BE HONEST, I did not have the best comprehension of what this "think time" entailed—I imagined Winnie the Pooh in his Thinking Spot and chuckled at how stupid he was portrayed. I probably looked similarly lost, trying to figure out how to think about the bigger picture, and eventually deciding I'd be better served by doing actual work.

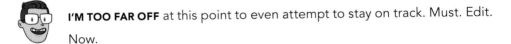

1:40 P.M.
Do brief face-to-face check-ins with your team.
(Also, no more caffeine from here on out; sorry.)

I'M TOO FAR OFF at this point to even attempt to stay on track. Must. Edit. Now.

I KNOW many of you reading this are used to just seeing the four of us on-screen, but there is a whole team of people that help us make our visions a reality. So I used this time to talk to our production team about planning a

Halloween party during a half day at the office as a way to say thanks to our staff for all of their hard work. Without them we wouldn't be able to release nearly as much Try Guys content!

Our first company photo! It took us accomplishing something to realize we should probably document the team.

SINCE MY WHOLE MORNING had already been spent on meetings, I used this time for classic water-cooler chat (note: we don't own an actual water cooler yet—we should chat about that). I asked my coworkers if they'd watched any cool videos lately and checked in on their significant others and/or pets. Somehow it turned into a very heated debate about whether or not kiwi is a valuable member of the fruit community. It is and you're wrong, Miles. As Kevin Lin told us, procrastination is good for the brain—it helps refresh and reset the clock before you dive into more work, and socialization is absolutely necessary to maintain sanity. Before long, twenty minutes was up and it was back to work.

I DECIDED the most effective way to do this was to go to each of our employees to speak to them on action items that need addressing. These moments would typically be stolen periodically, with no real structure, throughout the day, so piling them all into one concentrated window did sound like rational methodology.

Unfortunately, it soon hit me that the last time I had effectively conversed with producers, production assistants, and editors about important matters at hand was when I shot out a bunch of emails at 9:30 a.m. Since we're not your typical, somewhat removed CEOs and our opinions are needed for even the most minute decisions at this point in our young company, I felt like I had fallen behind since then. Now, it's not impossible to make these meetings work, but apparently it takes even greater care and foresight to ensure that when you send your morning directives they are thorough and consuming enough to last until the next time you're available to powwow. I adjust my feedback to ensure they can last without me for the rest of my CEO afternoon.

2:30 P.M.
Dedicated three-hour work block divided up with "timeboxing"—allotting a fixed, maximum unit of time for a preplanned activity, the way God intended it.

I JUST DID WORK. Fuck the boxes. (I think Steve Jobs said that.)

Right now we're working on our distracted-driving series, where we filmed ourselves driving drunk, driving high, driving sleep-deprived, and texting while driving. It's been a series we've wanted to make for years, but obviously every aspect of it is illegal, so we were never allowed to make it at our previous job. But now we're a small enough company that people aren't worried about what we do yet! In all seriousness, though, we get really excited about educational content that is also edgy and ridiculous. We're also interested in learning about the effects of different intoxicants, because there truly isn't a lot of science out there that compares them. The biggest challenge was getting a speedway that would let us do it . . . and to get the Los Angeles Police Department to give us an officer to speak on it . . . and to create something safe out of something completely unsafe.

To capture something this big in scope, we had about nine cameras on the ground for a few days straight, shooting tons of footage. And being precious artists, we didn't think it was possible for anyone to edit something this challenging except us, so we slowly chipped away at the project over the next few months. But we could never find the time to finish it. Finally we gave it to our best post team, and they not only finished the series, but they also did amazing work that we probably wouldn't have come up with ourselves. It was a huge lesson in prioritizing and delegating.

Oh, except for the fact that Eugene and I didn't have enough time to hand our edits off so we actually have to finish the editing ourselves and it's driving us nuts and it was a *huge mistake*. That's why I'm failing at the CEO schedule. I'm still editing.

OKAY, so I'm actually very excited about timeboxing. Here's how it works: I would work for twenty-five minutes straight and take a five-minute break. That would be one box. Then I planned out how many boxes I thought each task would take.

I had led all the preproduction and course design for the DUI series, so by this point it was my precious, $30,000-and-two-months-of-my-life-dear-God-I-hope-people-like-this-series baby. We split up the edits and I chose "The Try Guys Test Sleep-Deprived Driving" because I actually *am* sleep-deprived from caring for Wes. It was a large undertaking. In the video, we stayed up all night and then drove Keith's car on a closed-course to test what sleep-deprived driving was like. That meant there was a whole night's worth of cell phone footage plus the four different driving tests, each with nine different cameras rolling simultaneously. The problem is, it turns out watching us try to stay up all night was way funnier than I remembered and it took me forever to get to editing the actual driving because I was enjoying watching and cutting the sleepover footage so much. It started with about forty minutes of us dancing in animal onesies and by 3 a.m. I put a stuffed chicken in a diaper and set it down asleep in Wes's bed. I edited our night into a surrealist horror movie and it delighted me to no end. But I kept running over time on my twenty-five-minute time boxes, which defeated the purpose.

 **I DIDN'T REALLY** understand timeboxing at first, but Ned described it as breaking up work into units of time and trying to hold myself to it. Each box represents twenty-five minutes of work, with five minutes to get up and stretch my achy back, meaning I had six blocks to work with.

A decent chunk of box one was spent doing bathroom stuff. Sorry. I'm trying to be open and honest here and that's just what happened.

I spent box 2 and the remaining chunk of nonbathroom time box 1 meeting with our editor to hand off the DUI edit. And then the rest of the day turned immediately into a frantic blur. You see, we weren't just finishing these DUI videos, by far the biggest and most ambitious videos produced on the new channel; the rest of life kept drumming along. There were three other videos to be approved that needed thumbnails and packaging, emails from our agent about a pitch we're putting together, and, oh yeah, we're still writing a fucking book. To top it all off, we decided to release these videos leading up to the Streamys, the Oscars of the internet, a show we agreed to host. We have a real shit habit of piling on as many things as humanly possible all at once. Since my video was coming out last, I offered to be the swing man and fill needs that would usually be dispersed among the four of us.

Normally I stall as long as possible and wait for inspiration to hit. Timeboxing was there to say "uh-uh, bitch, get moving." It was like the feeling the night before a paper is due; it doesn't matter how you get there because someway, somehow, that shit's gotta be done by the time the sun rises, so chug that Red Bull and let's dance. Most of my time was spent going over notes from the Streamys, rejecting the script they wanted us to read and deciding to just rewrite it all (fun fact: the four of us wrote every word we spoke in that show, including an original song from Keith, original choreography from Eugene, a killer sketch from Ned, and a bomb-ass video plus some hot one-liners from yours truly). Blocks 5 and 6 were spent on editing video packages for the show as fast as my little fingers could go, and before I knew it the day was over and I was ready to collapse.

 **I TEND TO** be highly reactionary, as many creatives are, meaning I respond to what's most demanding in the moment and shine a spotlight on it as the rest of the world falls to black until the next unexpected project screams in the darkness and I swivel the spotlight onto it, and so on. This to-do was distinctly action oriented: I'd need to ignore all spontaneous distractions and switch gears regardless of how engrossing a project is.

As the editor of the first video of our DUI series (the drunk-driving premiere), my work sets the tone for the whole series, so I needed to finish the cut as soon as humanly possible. And that began with determining the graphics and animation style, and the actual point system in which we're penalized for traffic infractions in the series. Unfortunately, three hours of regimented work on a busy day is perhaps not the way our company is run. I had so much to accomplish with the video edit itself but I had to make a decision: because the graphics and point system affected the other guys' edits more immediately, I began designing and

sharing those ideas before actually cutting my own video. It essentially set my own personal work back but sped up our collective group work. Basically I spent these three hours deciding what the traffic cone graphic should look like and how much of a deduction we'd get if we ran through a stop sign, and it was worth it.

5:30 P.M.
Group dinner.

I HAD DINNER with my wife.

IF BY GROUP DINNER, you mean a group dinner with Wesley and Ariel consisting mostly of watching Wes smash berries on his cheeks, then yes, I had a group dinner.

I USUALLY WAIT to eat dinner at home with Maggie, so I spent the last thirty minutes of the official workday checking in with everyone and then setting my agenda for the next day. CEO day was over, but I liked how productive I was able to be and wanted to set similar goals for the following day. Also, I should wear turtlenecks more often.

IF THERE'S ONE THING you should know about our regrettable history with work-life balance, it's that there is no way in hell we would voluntarily have a group dinner on a weekday unless we were staying late on a project, because the Try Wives (yes, you heard me) would murder everyone. We see each other more than we see our other loved ones, so this was a nonnegotiable alteration: dinner would be on your own accord with whoever your most valuable one-on-one time is with. The last couple of hours I spend returning to my video edit.

7:45 P.M.
Go home.

I'M ALREADY HOME.

SIX THIRTY P.M. is bath time and bedtime for Wes. I really try hard to make it home for bath time and I am usually the one to put him to bed. I don't get to see him throughout the day so when I work late and he is already asleep I get a little sad! At 7:00 p.m. it was finally just me and Ariel again, so we shared a glass of wine and talked about our days.

WITH A FULL DAY'S WORK behind me, I was able to get home early, cook(!) dinner with Maggie, and join her for a walk with Bowie. We watched an episode of *The Good Place*, cleaned the dishes, and shared stories from the day. It felt quite adult and lovely.

SEVEN FORTY-FIVE P.M. feels like a more realistic average of when we'd drop everything to exit on a daily basis. Considering my commute grows to about forty-five minutes to get home, it dawned on me as I turn on NPR and listen to a recap of the day's significant world events that I had successfully stayed away from constantly checking in on news and social media, and my fingers instantly grew itchy with excitement to check my social blossoms.

8:30 P.M.
"Escort" electronic devices out of your room.

WHAT FAIRY-TALE LIFE is this CEO living. "Escort"??

WHILE I'VE NEVER called it a delightful term like "escorting," this piece of advice I actually already take to heart. Every night, I tuck my phone in my closet, far away from my bed, and try not to check it again. Sometimes I miss out on things, like one morning I woke up to a bunch of texts from Eugene asking me if I wanted to come out to a West Hollywood bar on a Tuesday night at 11:30 p.m. Putting my phone away helps me sleep better, though. And how do I wake up without an alarm on my phone, you ask? Two words: baby Wes.

THIS IS SUCH an adorable and quaint image. I'm going to go ahead and admit that I did not do this, but I did leave my phone facedown on the table and only mindlessly refreshed my apps like four times for the rest of the night instead of twenty.

THIS PIECE OF ADVICE is one I explicitly didn't heed—in fact, because I had been so successful at staying away from social media, I spent my first half hour at home scrolling through every damn platform I could get my hands on. It felt deserved. Knowing that it wasn't too difficult to go cold turkey in the office inspired this evening goal, but I'd come to find that when you're blasé and alone at home, avoiding social media is infinitely more problematic.

9:00 P.M.
Unwind by doing chores.
Or taking a walk outside without music.

ARE YOU FUCKING KIDDING ME? Chores. Chores?

I DID ACTUALLY put away my laundry because CEOs can't have their closets messy and it felt good.

I DECIDED to dedicate this thirty minutes to stretching and doing yoga, something I'd been struggling to work into my evenings but is desperately needed as I work on myself. Having a stretch sesh to bookend my day feels like a good compromise when I can't make it to the gym.

I DESPISE CHORES. But I have two dogs, so a walk outside was already in the cards for me. I made it extra-long and purposefully left my phone in the apartment, traversing multiple blocks, marveling at how often my pup Emma can poop for having such a petite frame. In a weird way, monitoring two dog buttholes for signs of shit was wondrously decompressing.

By the end of our hike, the combination of the extremely early morning workout, stress from adhering to our CEO itinerary, and what can only be described as caffeine depletion washed over me like a cavalcade of bricks, and I plopped my ass down on the couch, spent. I actually mused aloud: "I think I'm tired." This is uncharacteristic, especially for me at such an early evening hour, so I was tickled by the prospect of potentially being able to go to bed early without the woes of insomnia.

9:30 P.M.
Take a hot bath with Epsom salts.

 AM I A GRANDMOTHER?

 WOW, who knew that bath time was great for adults as well as kids? I plopped a bath bomb into a pool of steaming water and hopped right in. I am living the fucking dream right now. No wonder Wes loves bath time so much. I am the Richard Branson of bath time. These essential oils are sending me to space and back. I can't really imagine this as a nightly ritual but it was certainly a nice time to think and relax, while I lavished in the sweet scent of lavender.

 I DON'T EVEN HAVE a bathtub, nor do I have Epsom salts or know what that even is.

 THIS IS a hilarious idea that I had no intention of completing. I don't have a sexy enough bath, or Epsom salts, and on top of that, the idea of bathing as relaxation has never been attractive to me. Even luxuriating in a shower seems like an awful waste of my precious time and the earth's water.

Instead I eat dinner, which usually would be an enormous smorgasbord I'd collect from the nearby Whole Foods or a delivery order of *mukbang* that's far too large for one person to handle. Today was different, though, and the presence of my hipster avocado toast and Mark Wahlberg sandwich chugging down my intestinal track led me to quickly toss together a bowl of brown rice, a couple of fried eggs, and soy sauce. After I'd scarfed down the meal, I pumped a silent fist into the air. Three square meals for the first time in a very long stretch of shitty eating habits—if this CEO day has taught me anything, it's that a regular and balanced three-meal day is standardized for good reason. I felt positively refreshed.

10:00 P.M.
Change into clothes dedicated
specifically to sleep and nothing else.

 JUST CALL THEM PAJAMAS.

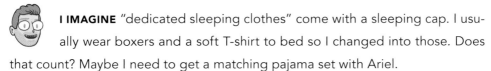 **I IMAGINE** "dedicated sleeping clothes" come with a sleeping cap. I usually wear boxers and a soft T-shirt to bed so I changed into those. Does that count? Maybe I need to get a matching pajama set with Ariel.

I SLEEP NAKED. So I enjoyed this part thoroughly, but I did get yelled at for walking by an open window.

 SO . . . I sleep in my underwear, if in anything at all. Pajamas or "sleeping clothes" make me think of white couples from the 1950s who slept in separate twin beds. Without going into any further detail—I'm basically naked from here on out. My sleep clothes are a birthday suit.

10:15 P.M.
Drink chamomile or lavender tea.

 I THOUGHT my clothes were only for sleeping! Are these now tea clothes?!

 OKAY, MOM, SURE.

 MORE TEA? Easy.

 THIS WAS a first for me, since the idea of tea, or any typically caffeinated beverage, for that matter, imbibed for relaxation instead of jazzification was not something I would have expected to be on this list. However, after noticing how uniquely slumberous I was feeling after restricting my coffee intake later in the day and the aforementioned three square meals, I dug up an old "Sleepytime" tea box.

Again, much of my aversion to some of these measures, like the same boring outfit and the sleeping clothes and evening tea, are due to me associating them with weird older individuals who maybe live in England and knit for kicks. But the tea did indeed make me more torpid, and I was yawning before I knew it.

10:30 P.M.
Write down the things that you're grateful for today.

WELP, my CEO day has been a complete and utter failure. I started out so hopeful. I had this nice breakdown schedule to follow, and then I totally fucked up every hour's goal. I should have known that trying to adapt to someone else's lifestyle in one day was not going to work. Especially right now in this weird time of "everyone is doing everything at this company." We are all CEOs right now. But also, none of us are. I guarantee none of the other guys will be able to stick to this, either.

I'M GRATEFUL that we own our own business! It's been a dream of mine since I watched *The Social Network*. No, but honestly, I have worked so many jobs over the years, and I have always wanted to have the control and autonomy, the high risk but high reward of calling all the shots. I'm grateful that I have my three best friends all in it with me, with everyone incredibly committed and passionate about building something big and exciting. I'm grateful that I have a hilarious, fascinating wife whom I love spending time with and an adorable baby who together ground me and make CEO day still feel like dad/husband/family day.

CEO DAY was stressful and not a total success from start to finish, but I took from it a ton that I hope to integrate into the normal flow of my work-life moving forward. All these methods are ultimately about productivity, because efficiency leads to balance. Balance in how you work, and, more important, balance in how you live. It's so easy to forget why we work. My happiness has been so hopelessly intertwined with my output that I'd forgotten why I do any of this to begin with. Life isn't about work, and success doesn't magically make you happier. I honestly feel like I need that knitted into a sign to hang over my nightstand.

I still love work and dare I say I'm obsessed with it? I think that's awesome. I love what I do, and I'm beyond fortunate to be able to look forward to work every single day. I love telling stories, and that will always be a part of me. But it doesn't have to be the whole of me. This experiment didn't dissuade me from wanting to work harder, it simply taught me how to work smarter. Along the way, it also reminded me that there are other things in my life just as important, if not more so. When I look back at my life fifty years from now, how will I have wished I spent my time?

I'M GRATEFUL that I was able to learn valuable insights, not only about how to work and lead a company more effectively, but also how I can improve all aspects of my daily life, since so many harmful habits are tied directly to the way you approach school or employment. Some of the more important insights were setting clear times for particular meetings and endeavors, scheduling our personal tasks more definitively, and limiting outside distractions such as browsing emails and social media.

On the other hand, as four guys who have struggled with maintaining a healthy work-life balance in the past, perhaps there's a deeper poignancy to be learned from this try. Being a successful CEO requires a certain amount of sacrifice. Perhaps there are times when that's necessary, and maybe there will be other moments when we should learn how to step away, relinquish some control, and value the betterment of our health and lifestyle. A balance between being the best bosses we can be while becoming better people, even outside of the office, should be aimed for, and if the CEO schedule was one rigid path to success, then we should learn how to forge our own unique one that allows for more twists and turns but still leads to the same goal.

10:45 P.M.
Go to sleep.

 GO TO HELL.

 FUCK YEAH, BOIIIIIIIII. I need it.

 AS YOU WISH.

 I CLIMB INTO BED, expecting for it to take forever, and think about how long Mr. Sandman will ignore me this time. Boom. I'm out like a light.

WHAT WE LEARNED

* Take care of yourself. What you eat and drink, and how much you sleep and exercise, can have enormous effects on your productivity.

* Set a schedule and (try to) stick to it. Having at least some structure in your day can minimize the amount of time you waste on Instagram.

* But also . . . procrastination is a good thing! Your brain needs a break every once in a while.

* Remember: you work to live, not the other way around. Thinking about *why* you are putting in those long hours working for the Man can give you much-needed perspective.

CHAPTER FIVE

Love

The original title of this book was *The Try Guys Are All Really Good at Doing Sex Stuff*, but our publisher told us it was a little too narrow and also "not true." Okay, fine. But when it comes to dating, the four of us have all been unlucky in love at some point in our lives. Fortunately, we've also been very *lucky* in love. Two of us are married. One of us is in a very serious, long-term, cohabitating relationship. And the other is Eugene.

Having a significant other really makes everything in life better. Food tastes better. The sun shines brighter. Except when you get into a fight with your siggy-oth (trademark), in which case everything gets much, much worse. Food tastes terrible. The sun, I guess in this analogy, turns dark and cold and everything dies. At least it can feel that way when things are not going well with your siggy-oth. So we're going to tell you about our breakups and makeups and all the ways we are *not* the ideal boyfriend/husband. It's going to be painful to explore the most intimate aspects of our love lives but we will do it so you can find that special someone in *your* life. Please just invite us to the wedding. Let's get siggy with it.

What's Wrong with Us

OH BOY, DATING.

For years, romance evaded me entirely. I wasn't exactly a "hot catch" growing up, despite the serious Dwight Schrute vibes I was giving off. My childhood was stuffed to the brim with unrequited love and one-sided crushes, which extended deep into my twenties. I filled my adolescence with as many sappy, romantic movies as time would allow, and I roamed the elementary school hallways wondering who would end up being the Sally to my Harry.

When I fell, I fell hard. I'm talking scribbling names in the corners of my notebook, role-playing fantasies with my stuffed animals, lying in bed and imagining what our future children would be like (one daughter, one son, and a few more children we adopt in later years). Usher came out with the song "U Got It Bad" when I was eleven years old and I was like, *Hot damn, Usher, you get me.* Months would go by, and despite hopelessly crushing on girls, I was always too afraid to actually say anything of substance to them. If movies taught me anything, it was that relationships are founded on big, sweeping declarations of love. But I seemed to miss the parts where the characters, you know, actually talked to one another.

In fourth grade it was Lisa Barkley. Lisa was the prettiest girl in class, with mesmerizing eyes, flowing blond hair, and a warm smile. A normal thing for me to think at that age, but admittedly uncomfortable to write about a child as an adult man. Lisa was dating Doug—everyone knew it, they were the hot couple of the year. But that wasn't about to stop me, because I *loved* Lisa, and I knew that she would feel the same about me. So in preparation for Valentine's Day—a little on the nose, I know—I convinced my mom to drive me to the strip mall so I could buy items to assemble into a gift bag for Lisa. I put together a basket filled with the best candy allowance could buy, with an oh-so-cute teddy bear sitting in the middle. If memory serves, I also gave her a handwritten letter, proudly revealing my feelings. Looking back, I can easily recognize this as a slow-moving train wreck, and shame on my mom for encouraging me.

I marched into school, a skip in my step and the cumbersome gift basket cradled in my twiglike arms. This was my moment. *The* moment. "Hi, Lisa," I heard myself squeak, a mix between that pained whisper you let out when your back hurts and the dying cry of a mouse in the clenched jaws of a housecat. She turned and faced me. I wished her a happy Valentine's Day and handed her my basket, which she accepted with a surprised smile. "Oh. Thank you," she said. *And then we never spoke of that moment ever again for the next eight years we were in school together.* Fucking swept her right off her feet, Yung Casanova.*

While Lisa accepted my gift, she did not jump into my imaginary red convertible so we could drive away together into the sunset. My romantic gesture fizzled and left me empty-handed, and that ember inside my heart dimmed. As it did in seventh grade when I tried the Valentine's Day sweep-her-off-her-feet-with-a-bear move again, this time with Jennifer D. Or in eleventh grade when I tried to score some weed for Wendy B. By the end of high school, I had to accept reality: grand romantic gestures are not my forte.

College would be different, I told myself. But years of quiet rejections encased me with a sheen of fear. I crushed from a comfortable distance, projecting what I wanted my crushes to be, but not getting to know them for the people they really were. I put all these emotional eggs in a basket, and when girls didn't just magically like me back, I was devastated. It was totally unfair, both to myself and to the girls I was attracted to, but that was my reality.

I got through college without ever entering into a real relationship. Look, I wasn't a total square. I had a lot of fun, and not totally infrequently. But when things got too serious, the emotional memory of rejection would take over and hold me back. To combat it, I applied a limit to my relationships—a firm do-not-cross threshold that protected me from any form of vulnerability but also served to stunt my growth as a person. I left college with a degree and an emotional debt that not even Sallie Mae wanted to collect. I went from hopeless romantic to just hopeless, and that's where I stayed for a few years.

In the absence of a relationship, I threw myself into work. The novelty of being single but busy worked well for a few years, but by my mid-twenties, I was, well . . .

---

* *Yung Casanova* is available as the follow-up mixtape to *Hebrew School Dropout*.

lonely. My dating life would follow a regular pattern: I'd decide to get back out there, re-download the apps, go on a series of dates for a few weeks, meet someone okay, watch as our relationship dissolved over the next few months, and then retreat into a cocoon of not dating where no one can hurt me. In the few dates I got, neither of us would prioritize the other. Most of the time women would ghost me, or sometimes I would get too busy with work and ghost them. If we couldn't find time for at least three dates in a month, I knew it wouldn't pan out. A cloud of insecurity pursued me: I didn't just dread that I was a bad partner, I was pretty damn sure of it. This overarching fear of rejection, or fear of disappointing someone if they ever expressed interest in me, pushed others away.

Closer inspection—and time!—has shown me that it all boils down to confidence. I was afraid to fail, and afraid that I wasn't good enough. Because, as we've covered, failing sucks. It hurts. It's awkward. It's embarrassing. But if you're too afraid to fail, then you're too afraid to live. So, at the tender age of twenty-five I decided to fail in dating as hard as I could. Mind you, this was almost three years before we solidified our Try Guys philosophy, *so I would like the record to state that I definitely invented this and deserve all the credit for this book.*

The plan was simple. I needed to put myself out there. The first step to failing at dating, it turns out, is to actually talk to people. So that's what I did—every weekend I made it my job to talk to one girl who I thought was out of my league. The way to meet new people, as it turns out, isn't all that different from the way you connect with friends in real life: ask questions, listen, and find common interests.

The first few rejections hurt like hell, especially when they were in public. When a stranger is not immediately receptive to you, it can be humiliating. It feels like everyone is watching you and that she is not just rejecting you, but your entire family and everything you hold dear. Your sweat glands start squirting their defense spray and your face turns that unique shade of red the body for some reason produces to advertise your ineptitude. But with each consecutive whiff, the impact softens.

Online dating was especially useful during this period. For some reason people still look down on dating apps, but I'm here to tell you they're amazing. We meet people where we spend most of our time, and in the 2010s we spend a

Seriously, who wouldn't swipe right on this stud?

lot of our time on our phones. There. Is. Nothing. Weird. About. Dating apps. Say it louder for the people in the back.

Yet Old Zach on dating apps (see a few choice Tinder photos at left . . . wow, we're really printing these?) was as high-strung as they come: scrutinizing every incoming message, hunting in their profile photos for clues, and endlessly drafting and redrafting messages in an effort to say the *perfect* thing to sweep them off their feet. Of course, my anxiety led me to achieve the exact opposite—with hours in between messages, I thwarted the chance of any semblance of flow. I was less concerned with connecting and more with just saying the "right thing," whatever that means. And worst of all, I was letting fear dictate my behavior.

Just as in real life, flirting on a dating app requires a reckless sense of abandon and an overall attitude of not caring. Not in the blasé, unaffected sense, but coming from a place where you're not just unafraid to fail—you actually welcome it with open arms! If you're anything like me, you probably forgot that dating is supposed to be fun. So have fun! Ask them their favorite Beyoncé song (everyone has an opinion about Beyoncé). Tell them an embarrassing childhood memory or see if you can get advice on an absurd fabricated problem, like there's a cat loose somewhere in your walls and you can hear it meowing at night. I dare you to find the limit. You're not going to scare someone away by saying one wrong thing, and if you do, then I can guarantee that you weren't going to make it past the first date together anyway. Both in real life and online, you have to learn how to not give a shit and just have fun.

I should take a moment to acknowledge that this strategy absolutely did not always work. But that's okay, because it helped me grow. Failing, and realizing my worst fears of rejection, showed me that it really isn't all that bad. Ultimately you rub some dirt on the wound and move on (and hope it doesn't get infected— please under no circumstances rub dirt on your real wounds). *Trying* to fail— intentionally going in without the aim of succeeding and just allowing myself to just have fun—ironically handed me the keys to success. For the first time in my life, meeting people was enjoyable, because I wasn't nervous about the outcome. Put another way, I learned to stop worrying about consequences and just live in the moment. Some nights I'd put on a fake accent and see how long it would take for people to realize I wasn't really Russian (drunk people have a terrible gauge for fake accents). Some nights were just about getting onto the dance floor and going nuts with my friends. Wouldn't you know, those were always the nights we made the most new friends. The more I tried to seem "cool," whatever that means, the worse the results. The moment I loosened up and allowed myself some fun, the world opened at my fingertips.

Not caring meant I found myself in more positive situations. It meant that I was only putting my best self forward, and all the wonderful aspects of my personality were finally able to flourish, untethered by the voice in my head that was afraid to be embarrassed. Over the course of a year, it stopped feeling so risky and scary. And look, this didn't just happen in a vacuum. It coincided with the rising popularity of our show, and being on camera definitely played a role in making me more self-assured and comfortable in my own skin. Getting a better fashion sense was also key, as you saw how hot I looked in chapter 3. All this effort ended up preparing me for the moment I was waiting for. When the girl of my dreams entered my life, I was ready.

When Keith Met Becky

WHEN I WAS a senior at Illinois State University (ISU), there was a freshman named Becky whom I was friendly with. At Christmas, my improv group, the ISU Improv Mafia (cool name, I know), threw a party called "Blastmas." We did a Secret Santa, but every single gift was booze. We had this bit where we would unwrap the gift pretending that we didn't know that it was alcohol, and then get really excited that it was our favorite alcohol. It was a silly excuse to have a party with too much booze, but it was still important that we wrapped it and made it a fun experience, because we improv folk liked themed events.

This being college, there were underage people there who had to figure out how to both buy liquor *and* get it wrapped. On the day of the party, people would sometimes show up at our apartment and drop off their booze, so it could be in the fridge and they didn't have to worry about it. My roommates liked Becky, so they invited her to Blastmas, and the more, the merrier, I thought!

Becky got someone to buy her booze, and when she came over to the apartment to drop it off, I asked if she was going to wrap it. "I don't have any wrapping paper," she said, and I snapped back with "Well you should get some and wrap it. *It has to be wrapped.*" There was some back-and-forth about how she didn't think it mattered and I told her that it did, that it was my party and that's how the party worked. She said it was hard enough for an underage person to get alcohol, and I said that's not an excuse. I could have been nicer, could have offered to help wrap it for her, but I chose to be a jerk instead.

I didn't think much of the exchange, but Becky remembered it apparently forever, and she held a grudge against me for the rest of the year and then the next year or two after that. And since the party was related to my improv group, I think she decided she would also hold a grudge against all the other dumb bits that we liked to participate in. To this day she still hates our stupid drink cheer "Zebra Stripes! Down the Pipes" and now that I think of it, I bet we did overwhelm her with that ditty throughout the party.

After graduation, I had both a whirlwind of a time and a very poor dating track record. I started touring with Mission Improvable, a comedy troupe, where we'd travel to colleges to perform shows almost every night of the week, only to have three days off and then head out again for a few weeks. The grueling schedule made it next to impossible to maintain a relationship and contributed to my breaking up with the girl I was dating at the time.

In 2011 I came back to ISU for the Improv Mafia funeral show, which is the last show for that year's seniors, and where they are roasted in a sweet sendoff. Sometimes alumni come back to roast the seniors as well. I did a bit where I imitated one of Becky's friends, who happened to be dating one of the seniors we were roasting. Somehow that silly portrayal, combined with a couple years of maturity and a nice haircut, was enough to change Becky's opinion of me. She told my friend she thought I was cute. I told my friend I thought Becky was cute. And then we were off!

I messaged Becky on Facebook and proceeded to court her the only way I knew how: sending her funny videos that I had made online—weird, low-production-value sketches, confusing comedy music videos, and long and poorly edited improv shows. What was I thinking? It says a lot about Becky that she was kind enough to go on a date with me even after that barrage of self-promotion.

The first few dates that Becky and I had were very sweet, but neither of us could read the other. I was sure she only kinda liked me, not *liked me liked me*, so I didn't make any real moves. I also only took her to hot dog restaurants. Then, after a few months of dating, I sug-

gested she celebrate her twenty-first birthday at a bar close to me, and then I didn't even show up! And one time I didn't walk her back to her train stop because I thought it was insulting to assume she needed someone to escort her. Basically, I almost blew it a hundred times.

On *my* birthday, I invited her to a party and in my mind I was like, "I don't know if she likes me but I'm gonna try to kiss her because it's my birthday." Apparently she also came to that party with the mind-set of "I don't know if he likes me but *I'm* gonna try to kiss him because it's his birthday." So at some point outside in the alley behind the party, we kissed for the first time, and I pulled away and romantically said, "I like how you have kind of a big mouth because I also have a big mouth."

Yes. That is what I said to her after finally kissing after two months of bizarre courtship. We've been together ever since.

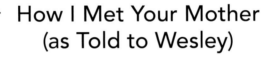

How I Met Your Mother
(as Told to Wesley)

featuring
ARIEL

HI, WESLEY. I know you're only a few months old, but it's time you hear *the* most important story in the world. Because without this story, you would not exist. Pay attention, because this is the story of how I met your mother.

We love you so much, little one. I'll be here, filling in the details.

Me and your mom met in Chicago in the winter of 2009 through a mutual friend named Becca. Becca was one of my close college friends and one of your mom's coworkers. On this particular night, Becca was having a birthday party, the kind of party where nine or ten people sit in a big circle and talk. I came into the circle and I was sitting on the complete opposite side from your mom.

Dad was late to the party. And he brought half a bottle of tequila.

 I could have sworn it was red wine.

 It was definitely tequila.

 Okay, so I brought a half-drunk bottle of tequila. Great first impression. Anyway, I sat down, immediately noticed Mom on the other side of the room, and thought to myself, "Who is that? I did not know Becca had such gorgeous friends." Eventually we started talking to each other, leaning forward across the circle, making everyone listen to our conversation. We learned about how we both loved to travel the world and both loved camping and being outdoors. Your mom had gone to high school in London and took a year off from college to hike across Costa Rica and I was fascinated by her. Over the course of the evening, little by little, I worked myself around the circle until I was sitting right next to her. I remember thinking she was so funny and charming and beautiful that I had to get to know her more. Yet, at that end of the night, I completely forgot to get her phone number because I wasn't really, you know, good at that type of thing. I remember the entire train ride back thinking I was so stupid that I was never gonna see this angel again. So that week I said to Becca, "Hey, your friend Ariel was . . . supercool. We should all hang out again." Becca took the hint and invited your mom to a group trivia night. And over the course of several trivia nights—

 It was one trivia night.

 Wasn't it a couple of trivia nights?

 I'm pretty sure there was one trivia night where you saved me a seat.

 Oh, yes, there was *the* trivia night where I got there fifteen minutes early and saved your mom a seat right next to me, and she got there fifteen minutes late.

It was a pretty big deal that you saved me a seat.

 I fended off six or seven people to sit in this spot. It was prime real estate. When your mom walked in she was behind her roommate, but when she spotted the open seat she did a full-on swim move, elbowed her roommate out of the way, and with a big smile said, "Hello, Ned."

 Do you remember the walk to the train?

 Of course! We were walking, just the two of us. And you said, "So, how are *you*?" In a way that I could tell that you cared about me. And I cared about you.

 I think this is a story about "When you know, you know."

 It's true. When you know, you know. I used to not believe in love at first sight. I thought it was a silly thing invented for romcoms and fairy tales, but truly, this was it. Our relationship moved very quickly. We were going on dates, and then we were going over to each other's houses nearly every evening of the week. Four months into dating, we decided to move in with each other. Now I know this is very quick, but we knew there was something special between us. That first summer, we went to South Africa together for the World Cup. I love our adventures together. We've been to Brazil, China, Hong Kong, Paris, and more—each trip an unforgettable adventure with my best friend. That first trip to South Africa was nearly a month long and it was a true test of our burgeoning relationship. There were sublime moments, like when we saw baby elephants walk by us, steps away from our rental sedan in Kruger National Park, or watching the sunsets from the cliffs of Cape Town. But there were also the challenges of being alone in a foreign country, like when I got food poisoning from some spicy lamb curry and your mom had to pull over for me to vomit every hour on the hour of a twelve-hour long car trip from Durban to Port Elizabeth. Or when our taxi driver took us on a shocking detour to a dusty shantytown in Soweto to drop off a package. I remember thinking during the trip, "If we can make it through this wild adventure, there is nothing we can't handle."

 That's when we knew.

 We got engaged only nine months into our relationship. I remember being at my desk at work and feeling this overwhelming sensation that if I got hit by a bus tomorrow, I'd want your mom to know the way I felt about her that day. I wanted to spend the rest of my life with her. This was something that I wanted to tell her *right now*. When I left work, I got a haircut and bought some flowers. I walked into a ring store and then walked out because it didn't quite feel right. To truly get the perfect ring, I would need to consult with your mom. And then I wrote her a long, tear-stained, completely incoherent note about how much she meant to me and how much I loved her. Then I put on a suit and I surprised her at her office. It was a Wednesday and Wednesday is date night, so she was expecting me, but she wasn't expecting a suit and flowers.

 I was wondering what was going on. It felt special. It felt different.

I barely held it together. Anytime I thought about her or thought about what she meant to me, I was about to start tearing up. She came out of her office and said, "Why are you wearing a suit?"

As everybody was watching through the window.

 And then I—

 And then you broke down.

 I lost it. I got down on one knee, and I told her how incredibly special she was to me and how I realized earlier that day that I wanted to spend the rest of my life with her. And I asked her to marry me. She said, "Oh my God, are you serious?" to which I replied, "Yeah," and then she said, "Of course, yes!" Then we just held each other for a long time. Later we called all of our family and told them the good news.

 They knew we had something special, too.

 I had just turned twenty-three when we got engaged. I was one of the first of my friends to get married, but it never felt strange, it never felt like it was too soon. It just always felt right and natural.

Just an expression of how we felt about each other.

We had a very long engagement, almost two years, which was so fun because wherever you go, when you say you're engaged, people are the most excited. We really savored that time. I remember we took a whole road trip up the California coast. Everywhere we stayed we said it was our engagement trip. We got several free bottles of champagne and *many* chocolates. By the time we actually got married at age twenty-five, other people were getting engaged and married as well. Really, when I think about every big milestone we've had, between getting engaged, getting married, getting a dog together, and having a baby together, I wouldn't say either of us was totally ready for any of it, we just knew that it was the right time.

We also just trust each other. Trust that we can do it. We always figure it out.

We do. That trust is so important. Wes, do you remember when I wrote about that horrific knee injury in chapter 2? That was actually only four months into our marriage. Your mom stayed with me for a month in Boston while I was recovering at my grandparents' house. It was very difficult and stressful for us both so early on. But we came out the other side stronger and even more in love. Relationships take work, they take effort; they don't happen naturally, and you have to continually make an effort to respect each other and be kind to each other. I have no idea who I would be and where I would be without your mom. She's so much a part of who I am, and we're just a part of each other.

I wouldn't want to know what I'd be like without your dad. And I wouldn't want to know what he'd be like without me.

We're so grateful we have each other. And Wesley, now we're so grateful we have you!

The 25-Year-Old Virgin

 I LOST my virginity when I was twenty-five years old. This revelation came as a shock to our viewership when I casually revealed it in the video "Which Try Guy Knows Eugene the Best?" Many assumed that I was a free-wheeling, promiscuous lush who must've had a tsunami of sexual partners. Quite the contrary: much of my delayed blooming was due to the adversity I dealt with when coming to terms with my sexuality.

First, let's get one thing *straight* (pun unintended): I have an inherently distrustful view of the concept of love. You might even go so far as to label me the anti-Ned. My parents' marriage was so unhappy and fraught with cultural politics and unnecessary sacrifice that when they divorced when I was in middle school, the first emotion I felt was relief. They were essentially expected to stay with one another, regardless of how they felt, because Asians are oftentimes raised with a sense of duty and position over personal preference. It was never fair to expect them to stay together if it was devoid of love. I can say with confidence that many parents I've met from more traditional cultures are simply "sticking it out" with absolutely zero passion left, if any was present to begin with.

Love, to me, could be a performative act, and it could easily be fallen out of just as easily as couples dive into it. I attend friends' weddings and am moved by the romance and the ceremony, but never have I believed that a pair's ties are invulnerable. Shit happens. People change. Bravo to those success stories, few and far between, blissful in their geriatric years—but I'm not banking on it.

To a queer teenager in the conservative South, I was mortified by my developing sexuality, paralyzed by the reckoning I was sure would rain fire upon me should my family or community ever find out. Already having to deal with my otherness as an Asian kid, I bottled up my urges and identity, using the excuse to both friends and parents that I wasn't interested in dating because I was too engrossed by my work and future career. I was, if anything, decidedly asexual to my peers, but behind closed doors, I was combating exceedingly awful thoughts about how hopeless my situation was. I was convinced I would be closeted forever and that hearts, something I already felt skeptical about, were not in the hand I was dealt. A few of my closest friends would find out by the time I was a senior and were wonderful confidants to entrust my problems to, but there wasn't much I could do besides keeping it under wraps and preoccupying myself with homework and hobbies. It was all spades for me as I shoveled a deeper, darker hole in my depressed mind that would serve as my hiding place until I came out after graduating from high school.

Since there was barely anyone I could talk to about this for years, the admission burst out of me when I visited my mother in Paris (where she lived after she divorced my father). She told my dad, and my sisters eventually found out as well. I went to college in the very gray area every LGBT person knows all too well: my parents weren't totally on board the rainbow train, mainly because they hadn't seen any "proof" of my sexual preferences. I wasn't sure how to act around the other young, virile people I was meeting anew.

One might assume that attending USC was the tipping point in my tragic tale of self-discovery, where I began dating and fell in love and started to finally experience all the magical, salacious things I gawked at on teen dramas. Although I did become infinitely more comfortable with my sexuality and found a lasting support system, as I encourage any LGBT students to seek should they be coming out during college, I was unexpectedly confronted with a racial discourse, as an Asian male, that I wasn't prepared to engage in healthily.

The predominantly white, cisgendered LGBT youth culture in LA was equally as damaging for me as a person of color as was getting picked on in the South. I was accepted into certain higher social echelons of gay friends because I was deemed both attractive and masculine enough, clearly the "exception to most LGBT Asian guys." I was prized for being antithetical to my community's deeply ingrained racial-sexual tendencies. I was tall, wide-jawed, straight-acting, and aggressive—nothing like the preconceived notions many of my new acquaintances had about Asian men. The unchecked racism at the time in the West Hollywood parties that served as the environment of my coming out further pushed me into a dark mental place. I was suspicious and defensive: when anyone asked me out on a date, I would assume an underlying racial component to their attraction that led me to turn them down.

I refrained from dating at all until I was twenty-four, and even then I technically only went on a few first dates. If Texas fucked me up, Los Angeles fucked me over. But by the time I joined The Try Guys, I was as relatively well adjusted as someone who spent most of their life refusing even the faintest glimmer of love can be. By relying on my talent and carefully crafted, charming persona, I had navigated most social and professional situations without letting them know I was a virginal, conflicted, depressed shell of a human. But in a strange twist of fate, that persona I convinced myself I was engineering was, in fact, my real magnanimous self simply emerging from his cocoon, and an entire life of bottling up my feelings burst to the foreground as I worked out and resolved my issues through video.

LOVE

When Zachary Met Maggie

THE NIGHT I MET my girlfriend Maggie was the true embodiment of "luck favors the prepared," which itself is a corollary of "fortune favors the bold," which I believe is the old tagline for Doritos. She approached me at a gay bar—the Abbey in West Hollywood. More specifically, in the shared coed sinks outside the bathrooms of a gay bar.

Our eyes met, and I knew my night was about to change.

"You don't know this yet, but we're going to get married. I'm Dara."

Huh?

Right, so that wasn't Maggie. It was a girl named Dara whom I had never met before. Dara, as it turns out, was a fan of The Try Guys, and a very friendly (and forward!) one at that. I believe my super suave response was "Oh . . . really?" Then another girl, Shannon, approached. She and Dara had met in the bathroom and become instant best friends the way only young women seem capable of. It's pretty remarkable. Shannon, as I learned within fifteen seconds, was here visiting a friend and was celebrating a breakup but maybe shouldn't have taken a tequila shot from the bartender in the banana hammock with the nice abs. Behind them was *Maggie*—the most confused person I had ever seen in my life. What the hell was her best friend (Shannon) and new bathroom BFF (Dara) doing talking to me at the bathroom sink? (People often ask if Maggie knew who I was when we met, and the answer is no. I was just some weirdo in a bathroom.) I had never seen someone's face scrunch up into a question mark before. She was beautiful, scrunched face and all.

Neither of us remembers what we talked about that night. We've been back to that bar since and we don't even understand how it's possible that we *did* talk—it is so impossibly, overwhelmingly, aggressively loud in there. But something I said must've worked. We spent the next hour locked in conversation.

When the guys saw Maggie they quickly understood why I'd gone missing. As the lights flashed on to tell people to start their sloppy migration home (though we were both sober . . . I know pointing that out makes it seem like more of a lie, but we were), Maggie grabbed my hand to lead me through the crowd. Whenever

I bring this up she says it wasn't because she liked me; she just didn't want me to get lost. I counter that the fact she didn't want me to get lost proves she was totally into me from the start. Take that! (She probably wasn't, but a boy can dream.)

Our early relationship was a blur. Normally I was one to "play the game"—wait a few hours to text back, so as not to seem too needy. With Maggie, though, I threw all that out the window. I liked her. A lot. Plus I was playing the role of this confident guy, so I just went for it. Also, games are stupid and they never work—just be genuine. I texted her the morning after I met her. We had our first date two days later. We kissed for the first time and held hands on the way to dessert. I remember I made this joke about not wanting to give her my jacket because then I'd be cold. Truth be told, I still think it was a totally hilarious reversal of classic gender norms that empowered her as a self-fulfilled woman, but apparently she thought I was kind of a dick for that. Hey, you win some and you lose some, and with luck you learn to tell better jokes.

After four months, I told her I loved her. I remember the day, because we went to the beach—a big deal for me because I find sand to be a nuisance (it's tiny rocks and it gets everywhere and I don't understand what the big whoop is). Also, Pokémon Go had just come out and I caught an Electabuzz while sunbathing, a huge deal at the time. I don't know that I actually started with "I love you." I'm pretty sure I hid my face under a towel and said "I think I'm falling for you." She laughed and said the same back, and only

then was I able to confidently say the words I'd never said to anyone before. After that, I didn't have anything to fear ever again.

Maggie changed my life. She taught me what it means to love and to be loved, and has filled my life with jubilation and purpose in a way I've never felt before. We share a passion for live music and travel and eating our way through cities. And best of all, we have compatible food allergies—two mutated weirdos perfect for each other. She's the greatest thing that's ever happened to me, and I'm grateful every single day that I decided to go pee the night we met. Meeting her allowed me to finally close the previous chapter of my life and start writing the next one.

If you can't love yourself,
how in the hell you gonna love somebody else?

—Ru-fucking-Paul

Long Distance, Short Fuses

BECKY AND I have been together for seven years, and I'd say our relationship is the result of a very difficult "try." In 2013, at the tender age of twenty-five, and two years into dating Becky, I decided it was time for me to move from Chicago to Los Angeles. We had the expected heartache and stress in the months leading up to the move, and I totally broke down on my last day with her in Chicago. We were going to try long distance for a year, until Becky was ready to move herself.

We started out the first month with lots of calling. We'd do the normal exchange of how our days went and how much we missed each other, etc. At some point early on we realized that talking on the phone only bummed us out. For us, it put more focus on how lousy it was for our relationship, so we dialed it back to two to three times a week and more constant texting instead. It made things a little better, but the sadness over not seeing each other really hurt. As anyone who has ever done long distance can attest, the time difference can be a relationship minefield. Becky would call me at midnight her time on a Friday after going out, but it was ten for me so I was only beginning my night. Then there's this whole "Why are you going out and having fun instead of talking to me" sort of convo that couples have, an agonizing exercise I wouldn't wish on my worst enemy. We fought from time to time and had some of those long silent moments on the phone where it's clear both sides are hurt and unsure what to do. And sometimes there's nothing *to do*. You just have to work through that pain and awful distance. Long distance is supertough but having an end date to look forward to makes it a little easier. It's a light at the end of a really shitty tunnel.

In all the years we've been together, we've only had a few big fights, which came out of arguments that escalated too far because of other stressors in our lives. Becky had a career change shortly after coming to LA, which took her back to school. She at times felt like she lacked direction, and I was superstressed with the trajectory of my online video career. Sometimes these issues made us bicker with each other because we both felt overwhelmed by our new circumstances. I've learned, and am still learning, to treat each argument with care. Sometimes you should just agree with someone who is upset even if you think they're wrong. And sometimes you should accept you are, in fact, the wrong one and—even though it's hard to admit—you probably just should apologize. What's most important for me and Becky to remember is that we're a team, and even though we aren't perfect, we've grown to understand one another's faults and know how to either not let them bother us or avoid bringing them to light.

MOVIN' ON IN

Moving in together is a big moment in any relationship, but for Becky and me, we were just so happy to be together again. However, we did learn a few things about cohabitating that we want to share with you:

* You're going to have to clean up after one another. Accept that. Don't try to make it a competition, either. There will be times when it feels like you're the only one doing laundry or dishes or taxes or oil changes or whatever. *Suck it up.*

* The "what should we have for dinner" conversation just became your life now. You'll have 95 percent of dinners together moving forward. Choose new recipes and restaurants often, and push each other to try new things.

* If and when you see that your partner is upset, listen to them and ask if they want your help. Sometimes people just need to be upset and offering a solution isn't . . . the solution. It's going to be hard, but if you're both well intentioned, it will be okay.

* Most of all—have fun with your new roommate for life! (Hopefully.)

A Lifetime of Commitment

THERE'S A REASON that I talk about Ariel so much. She is the love of my life, my best friend, and the most special person in my world. She's funny, beautiful, charming, intelligent, and incredibly talented. But what you may not see on camera is how strong and supportive she is. She is my rock. She keeps me grounded. When the entire outside world is a maelstrom of stress, she is a sanctuary of love and peace. We rely on each other so deeply. She makes the good times that much sweeter and the bad times a little easier. After nearly a decade of being together, I've learned that the true foundation of a relationship is daily commitment, love, and respect for each other.

I sometimes see online comments about how our relationship and love for each other is so "perfect." While I appreciate the kind words, believe me, every relationship is tumultuous, messy, and real. It's got flaws and blind spots that a cute photo or a glossy filter doesn't ever see. We've had really difficult times, through Wes going to the NICU or my knee injury or Ariel's night classes for grad school or my midnight comedy shows or when we got evicted from our sublet when we first moved to LA (for subletting, ironically). Under the surface and through all the difficult times, it takes hard work. On our wedding day we made vows to each other, but each morning when we wake up we remind ourselves of those vows all over again; a wedding lasts a day, but a marriage lasts a lifetime.

After Wes was born, it got harder to focus on each other. Suddenly we didn't always have enough time or energy to connect with each other. When you're holding an infant, it can be difficult to have a deep conversation. So we had to make time. During the day, when both of our energy levels are high, we find someone to watch Wes and then go out to lunch together. It's a little different from our Wednesday date nights because this is dedicated time to work on our relationship. We almost treat it like an appointment. How's it going, *but like how's it actually going*? How can we each be more supportive? Are there difficulties

LOVE

197

we're having that we haven't been able to verbalize? How can I be the best partner for you? It's a focused environment where we're both 100 percent present. It was a little awkward at first to be so honest so quickly, but over time we've come to look forward to it as a time where we can address the issues that may get swept under the rug during day-to-day life.

I've heard the saying "Never go to bed angry," and while I think that is great advice in theory, it's nearly impossible once a kid enters the picture. The evening is when we're the most tired and least able to listen and process information. So if Ariel and I are having a disagreement at night and something is left unresolved, we make a point to talk about it in the morning, when we're fresh. As long as we don't let whatever it is get forgotten, we're much better equipped to resolve it together when our energy levels are high.

I love and care for Ariel so deeply that I can hardly put it into words. She is the single most important person in my life and I was forever changed the moment I met her. I don't know where I would be without her and I'm so grateful that the foundation of our relationship is rock solid. I think the mark of a strong marriage is being cognizant of your issues and actively working on them. Getting through the good times is easy, but it's getting through the tough times that really forges a strong marriage. Because Ariel and I have been through so much and come out the other side more in love than ever, I know there's nothing we can't handle.

The Grinch

THE EUGENE that people first saw online, with his dry, sardonic humor and dauntless posturing, was not necessarily an act: it was the identity that I had developed in order to directly confront and combat my raging internal war. That Eugene, born out of necessity, became the basis for my more fully realized, moderate, current self. By being ruthless, inappropriate, darkly comical, and devil-may-care, I garnered the courage to embrace my work as an on-camera personality. On another level I was able to avoid the opportunity for relationships or romance entirely, because anyone who came into my orbit would receive immediate signals that I was *not to be fucked with*. Like many artists, the most distinct, relatable parts of my personality were forged from my tormented process of constantly being "othered," while reinforcing the notion that I am both incapable of giving and receiving actual love.

I eventually did find a way to entrust myself into someone else's care and affection, and that relationship has emboldened my passions and philosophy on this subject for the better. But I regret to admit I still have doubts. I simply have never envisioned any relationship being able to stand the test of time, so is it really possible I will be some glorious, Shakespearean exception?

With the influence of the other Try Guys, I can attest that I'm no longer as vehemently against lofty devotion ideals, and watching Ned and Ariel, Keith and Becky, and Zach and Maggie manage their relationships with steady, unabashed adoration has softened my Grinch heart, maybe making it grow the tiniest bit. Although the rampant PDA the Fulmers exhibit icks me out to the bone, I am all the better for being balanced by friends, who are not only robust devotees of true love but shining examples of its very existence.

A BRIEF HISTORY OF TRYING

The King James Bible was first published in England in 1611 and was an instant hit. But a reprint that was published in 1631 had an eensy-weensy typo. One of the Ten Commandments is listed as: "Thou Shalt Commit Adultery."

Learning to Be a BF

RELATIONSHIPS ARE ALWAYS a work in progress. The idea that true love is easy and effortless is some fabricated romcom nonsense; being in a relationship is quite possibly the hardest thing you'll ever do and it requires constant work. Four months ago, Maggie and I moved in together. We share a beautiful fluffy son/dog. We talk about the future and, if all goes according to plan, are in it for the long haul. I found my person and we're as happy as two people can possibly be, and it blows my mind basically every single day. I wake up, look at her, and wonder how I haven't messed it up yet.

Growing up, I had a totally twisted view of intimacy. I imagined falling in love as the whirlwind of meeting someone new, the fireworks of your first kiss, the thrill of getting to know each other, and the electric nausea of saying "I love you" for the first time. But now that I've been in a relationship, I realize those moments aren't love at all. Love—*actual love*—is made up of a million "unromantic" milestones, like the first time you ask the other to pop that pimple on your back, or when you debate for days over what color bedsheets to buy. Love isn't the first time your eyes meet across the dance floor, it's the first time you fart in front of each other (not at the same time, that'd be nuts). Moving in together presented

the perfect opportunity to deepen our intimacy. I've shed the emotional weight of my past and found the greatest girlfriend in the world, *but . . .* as we enter this new stage together I'm fucking really terrified again. Now is the time for me to evolve as a human—to take that next step as a boyfriend and as a person. And honestly, I really feel like I'm lacking the tools necessary to be a decent life partner.

It really comes down to feeling like I'm not good enough. I think about the image of a family man—of a lover, partner, provider—and I'm not it. I'm twenty-eight years old but I still feel like a kid a lot of the time. I barely know how to take care of myself let alone how to take care of another person. This feeling of not being good enough rears its ugly head in several facets of my life, but usually it's just me versus me. In this case, it's something that threatens to impact my relationship. I think about my trepidations about taking the next steps, and it really seems to boil down to feeling like I need to get right before I can take care of someone else. I want more than anything to be that person—to be that person for us—so I know I've got some work to do.

Basically I'm a great boyfriend but a lousy roommate, and part of moving in together has included finding ways in which we're not immediately compatible. I'm told that's incredibly normal, but that didn't make it any less shocking. Maggie isn't just a neat person—she's the kind of person whose mental well-being relies on order in the house. To say I don't care about staying neat doesn't quite capture it—I'm just not even aware of it. I'm like a baby who lacks object permanence—if I don't see things I forget I own them. Conflict brews. This is the simplest of possible disputes (just clean up your shit, Zach; *yeah I know*) but it has predictably led to our first real fights as a couple.

I am also aware that I'm prone to being, as the French would say, totally up my own butt. It's really easy for me to get consumed with my work and I've had times where all I'm thinking about is myself. It's something I've been working on but it remains a terrible trait as far as coupledom goes. Maggie is the absolute most important thing in my life and I'm aware that there are times I could be better at putting her first. We're not talking about those grand romantic gestures I was obsessed with as a kid, we're talking the little things. Small gestures every day that remind her how much I love her.

When sitting down to write this book, I had to ask myself how my relationship could improve. At first, my puffer-fish response kicked in and I took it as a direct attack, both from myself and from our publisher. But the more it sat with me, the more that question revealed itself as a universal prompt applicable to anyone in a relationship, romantic or otherwise. Every connection in your life requires nourishing, and there's always room for improvement. You can't grow a plant without watering it—trust me, I've accidentally killed every plant I've ever owned. After close inspection, it was pretty clear what I had to do.

Decent Proposal

IN THIS DIGITAL AGE, it's much easier to drop hints to your boyfriend that you want him to propose. However, I was still mostly oblivious. I would turn on my computer to a Pinterest page called "preeettttyyyyy" that was just pictures of engagement rings. I'd think to myself, "Why is Becky always on Pinterest on my computer?" and close the tab and get back to my normal computing. *I know.*

After four years of dating, she asked me straight, "Are we gonna get married or what?" I was like, "Yeah, it seems like we are," and she was all, "Then why haven't you gotten me a ringggg," and I was like, "I don't know what kind of ring you want," and then she calmly said, "I'VE BEEN LEAVING AN ENGAGEMENT RING PINTEREST PAGE ON YOUR COMPUTER ONCE A WEEK FOR TWO YEARS." To which I said, "Oh. I just thought you liked Pinterest."

I started looking for a ring in earnest, but I didn't know what the hell I was doing. I asked my friend Hillary for advice and she had a friend who is a "ring broker." I should have known that meant "she will bring expensive rings" but I didn't, because I had no frame of reference. It's not like when you watch *Price Is Right* and you know that Jif peanut butter is like four bucks because you've seen the price in stores all your life.

Nonetheless, I met with the ring broker (always following our failosophy of consulting with experts!) and bought a beautiful ring I knew Becky would love. My plan was to propose around Christmas because we had planned to visit both families over break. I had the ring with me for the trip, but then her grandpa got sick and it just didn't seem like a good time to propose. It was a hard time for her family, so I kept the ring a secret.

We came back to LA, and so did the ring, secretly living in a specific part of my backpack. I checked that pocket *constantly* to make sure I didn't lose it. The next available time was around Valentine's Day, but that seemed cliché. And then the postponing of it just made it harder and harder to figure out what to do and how I could make it a big romantic thing. I wanted it to be a special memory for her, even though her only request was that she "wasn't wearing, like, sweatpants or something."

Then it was March, and she brought up why I hadn't proposed and I had to maintain a poker face. I tried to make it seem like I hadn't even thought of it.

In April, I figured I should try another angle. That angle was "Just pick the next holiday and figure it out." So I told Becky that for Easter it would be fun to do an Easter egg hunt, just the two of us. I woke up at 3 a.m., hid some eggs around our living room with candy and cute phrases, and then hid one egg that was impossible to find to ensure it was found last.

We woke up Easter morning, and I sent her on the little quest. She found all the eggs, plus the ones with clues to bigger boxes of candy placed around the house. I said there were fourteen eggs, but she had only found thirteen and needed to try harder. Finally, I knelt down as she dug out the last egg and opened it, and I asked her if she wanted to get married. She said *yes*, beaming, and then looked at the ring and said, "Oh my God. How much did this cost?" I said, "Let's just say it's our family heirloom now."

Also, since we went straight from bed to egg hunt, neither of us had put on any pants yet, so technically Becky wasn't "in, like, sweatpants or something."

And now . . . we're married! It was the most fun wedding ever. Each Try Guy really played his part. Eugene fixed so many broken boutonnieres and floral arrangement issues behind the scenes. Zach was running around greeting family members and shooting video. Ned, beaming with pride as another Try Guy was finally about to achieve married status, was checking in with me and making sure my family was relaxed and having fun. Having them there, along with my best men Brian Wohl and Marc Muszynski, and my brothers, was really wonderful. We all knew that this was a big emotional moment for Becky and me, but it was also one for The Try Guys. We'd been coworkers and best friends, but groomsmen is such a milestone moment in a friendship, and having them there made the day that much better.

In my vows I promised to continue to be Becky's best friend. Reminding each other that we are best friends and that we should treat each other as partners has been a key to our success. Marriage is both a relationship and a friendship. It's a bunch of little puzzles and efforts. It's . . . *a lot* sometimes. But it's worth it, and I must say, having someone to share this crazy life with is pretty amazing.

Wednesday Date Night

 ARIEL AND I have a date night once a week, and usually on Wednesdays because it's right in the middle of the week. We've been doing it since we first started dating and it's the highlight of my week!

Usually we go out to dinner. We love trying out new restaurants and savoring different types of food. It's a few blissful hours where we stare into each other's eyes like we're the only two people in the world. When we're feeling more adventurous we'll do a picnic. When we're feeling cozier, it could be as simple as sharing glasses of wine on the deck. It doesn't have to be anything fancy. Doing something big like a concert or gallery or event we usually save for the weekends and we often go in a group with friends. But our weeknight date night is always special because it's just the two of us.

In one of our infamous first videos, "Guys Recreate Kim Kardashian's Butt Photo," Zach asks, "Where's Ned?" And Keith says, "He went on a date with his wife." And everyone laughs. That part is true; I had to leave early. This was while Keith was rubbing oil on Zach's body.

 You missed out on a good oily time, bro.

 What can I say, date night is important!

When Ariel was pregnant, we realized that so many of our favorite date night activities involved drinking wine. It was difficult to go to our usual spots but not drink, so we ended up trying out and discovering new spots that didn't serve wine. And they were just as fun!

The baby has made some of the logistics around going out in the evenings more difficult because of the dreaded process of finding a babysitter. Recently Eugene, someone who is pretty anti-baby, watched Wes for the first time. He walked in wearing a suit and walked out wearing an unbuttoned shirt covered in spit-up. Even though Eugene is skittish around babies, I would absolutely let him babysit Wes again. Same goes for Keith or Zach. It takes a village and we need all the help we can get. Luckily, both our sisters now live in LA as well, so usually one of Wes's aunties babysits while we get to spend time together. Wes loves his aunties. And he loves his Try Uncles too!

One of my absolute favorite dates with Ariel took place in Chicago very soon after we first started dating. We had plans to go see *Avatar* in IMAX 3-D, but it was sold out. The evening may have ended right there, but instead we ate crab cakes,

 drank chardonnay, and laughed at each other's silly jokes in British accents. Then we noticed that a DePaul University homecoming dance was being held in an upstairs atrium that same night. Being young and brash, we attempted to crash it. Pretending to have stepped out for a second, we checked our coats and walked right past the ticket tables like we'd been there for hours. We got halfway across the dance floor when I felt a tap on my shoulder and a security guard said, "Do you have tickets?" and in some of the quickest thinking I may have ever done in my life, I replied, "Oh yes, of course, they already took our tickets at the other entrance." He and I stared at each other for a few long, cruel seconds. Then he bought it. "Okay, have a nice night." And we did. We danced like no one was watching for approximately two hours and forty-two minutes plus previews until the next showing of *Avatar* in IMAX 3-D.

You know you're in love when you can't fall asleep because reality is finally better than your dreams.

—*Dr. Fucking Seuss!*

Zach Tries a Romantic Gesture!

MAGGIE AND I moving in together, to what can charitably be called a fixer-upper apartment, coincided with The Try Guys launching our new company and YouTube channel. I was the busiest I've ever been in my life at a time when so much needed to be done to make our new apartment a home. Maggie is a registered nurse who puts in three overnight shifts a week. That meant that during all the repairs and furnishing and deliveries, she was the one who was home and taking the lead. It was easy for me to justify it: I'm incredibly busy, I'm not good at this stuff . . . all the obligatory defenses. But Maggie took on that burden without ever complaining. In my sea of responsibilities, I'd found myself neglecting my most important job of all: being a great boyfriend.

So, I decided to tackle a week of sweet and selfless gestures, putting her first and making time for her no matter what. For this endeavor, I'm focusing on things that I totally and completely suck at: decorating, organizing, cooking, planning. . . . I do realize I'm just listing out basic human functions, but that should give you an idea of the place I'm coming from. The goal is not only to surprise Maggie with things she doesn't expect, but to really give her the things she deserves. I chose things that, in an ideal world, should just become commonplace in my behavior. And in doing this, I hope to evolve as a boyfriend, because if I don't, it's only so long until she realizes she can do better.

The plan: Maggie is working three overnight shifts in a row at the hospital, which gives me ample time to pull off some fun little surprises. I want to do all the things she normally handles in the house—things she does for herself, things she does for me, and things she does for us. And then I'll throw in some things neither of us does for good measure: Meal prep, finish some house decorating, shower her with surprise treats, and end the week with a romantic home-cooked dinner.

Ready? Game on.

To start, I wanted something that would alleviate stress from Maggie's life. I had never meal prepped for myself before, which means, of course, I'd never meal prepped for another person, either. Cooking for Maggie would be a gesture equal parts sweet and practical, and would save her from whatever horrid cafeteria food she'd otherwise be subjected to. Plus, when we moved in together we made a pact to start cooking more meals, a promise I'd yet to fulfill. This gesture was my way of telling her I was committed to our shared goal and that I was going to take time in my life to make it a priority. To make *us* a priority.

As it turns out, I had no idea what meal prepping is. I thought you cooked one thing, but then magically you were left with four different meals. Like, you cook chicken and dice all the same veggies, but then it yields a taco bowl, a stir fry bowl, a salad, etc. I'm not sure how that would work . . . probably witchcraft. But apparently, *nooooooo*, meal prepping is just making a ton of one food and separating it into different bowls. Which is so stupid. Why is there a name for that? That's not meal prepping. That's having leftovers. If that's meal prepping, I've *only* ever meal prepped. It's insane how stupid I am considering how smart I am.

So there I was in the supermarket, an alien visiting earth and trying my hardest to just act cool and not get noticed for being a complete imbecile. It took me a full earth hour to find all the ingredients I was looking for. Keep in mind, I chose the simplest recipe I could find for stir fry and vegetables (baby steps). I unloaded at home, and that's when I realized about half the things that took me so long to track down were things I already owned (still struggling with object permanence). Also, I *didn't* own a pot big enough to boil pasta. So it was back out, this time to Target.

Maggie. Loves. Target. It's her happy place. I promise this isn't an ad, but she's a #TargetGirl. You know, the kind of person who goes there to clear her mind. Not me: even the idea of shopping makes me anxious. Normally I would beeline to an employee and ask to be pointed to the item I need, not bothering to look at the LARGE SIGNS dangling over every aisle. But since I was at Target to shop for Maggie, I wanted to shop like Maggie. I'd walk around and let the store find *me*. And then maybe I could learn what she loves so much about this place, so next time we come I can live in the moment and enjoy it with her.

I found the pot pretty immediately, but I luxuriated in my experience and ended up finding a ton of other great things we needed for the house: string lights and command hooks for the back patio, a fetch toy for Bowie, kitten-print pajama pants (those were for me), some decorative fake plants, and some wall art. That last one was a risk—we've certainly disagreed on art in the past but I was confident this one fit squarely in the snug peapod where our taste Venn diagram met. Also, with Target's amazing thirty-day return policy, you don't even need a receipt, so there's nothing to lose! Shop smart. Shop Target. (Not an ad.)

By the time I got home, it was 10:30 p.m. and I got to cooking, which only took me four times as long as the recipe suggested. *Liars*. My packaging of the meals didn't quite match the pictures online . . . it was like if someone put all the ingredients in a bag and shook it up real good. But I was done and had four equally portioned meals set aside for her, and my chef's sampler nibbles told me that it was pretty damn tasty despite some small missteps. It turns out, love was the secret ingredient all along. Awwwww.

I cleaned up the dishes and tidied up so that Maggie would return from shift to a lovely home. I created a bundle from the fake plants and stuck the branches in a large empty glass vase we had (wow, Zach, look at you go!) and made a delightful pumpkin vignette by the front door. There was a dumb little grin on my face the whole time. I was doing things I absolutely hated, but I was doing them for someone I loved.

When I surprised Maggie with her prepped meals the next morning, *I* started tearing up. Holy shit, I'm such a loser. But I was emotional. It felt like saying "I love you" for the first time all over again, but this time I was saying it with my actions.

The burnt salmon.

She didn't tear up but she did laugh at me for crying, which is the appropriate reaction. There's a reason I love her. But she was touched by all the gestures, and the big hug I got really made the whole thing worth it. She didn't mind all the mistakes in my cooking, and she certainly had some notes on my decorating, but the warmth my actions commanded almost canceled out the imperfections. Which is a relief because the next day I totally burned our salmon (how's that even possible, you might ask, to which I'd respond I'm a pretty special breed of human).

What struck me is that she tried to tell me this was all unnecessary. That the meal prep was so sweet and thoughtful but that I shouldn't feel like I have to do things like that for her. But of course I don't feel like I *have* to do these things for her. I *want* to do these things for her. When you're in a relationship sometimes it's the selfless, "no reason" acts of kindness that are most impactful in really expressing how you feel.

The next day, I hung the new art in our apartment. I learned an important lesson about how stud finders work and the significance of drywall, but nothing a little plaster can't fix. Turns out my floors are slightly sloped, meaning that mystery bubble you use to level things is totally useless in my home, so I just had to eyeball it. I ran out to Maggie's favorite ice cream shop and stocked the fridge with vegan fudge and rosé frosé (I may or may not have snuck a small bite of both . . . to make sure it was to her liking of course).

Ironically, a long weekend of preparing things for Maggie put me behind at work. My meal prep was listed as a forty-five-minute start-to-finish meal, and I managed to spend like six hours on it. I wish I were kidding. Shopping at the home goods store, hanging photos, realizing they're not level, taking down the photos, hanging them again . . . trying and failing miserably to string lights along our balcony so we could have our romantic dinner outside . . . that took me an entire day.

But the real lesson I've learned is more important: it's not about stopping everything I'm doing and throwing my life out of whack to make her happy (she never asked for that and would never allow it). Instead it's about finding ways to make some of these habits stick and to work sweet gestures into the flow of everyday life. Once the long weekend was over, I wasn't done. Just as my job and my health require dedicated focus every day, so too does my relationship, and that's so much bigger than anything I could fit into this book. It's the little things: I now wake up earlier and take care of all the morning dog chores before I go to work. I do her laundry without being asked, and only occasionally destroy her delicates. I surprise her with lunch when she wakes up the day after a night shift. Or I even work in a five-minute foot rub before I run off to work every morning. (I gave my first one last night but will spare you the details of my girlfriend's feet. I did watch a YouTube video to try to get better and look forward to having bizarre "suggested videos" for the rest of time.)

I've learned that part of being in a relationship is *practicing selflessness*, and there's a balance to that. Sometimes doing things for Maggie at the expense of my own time is kind of the whole point, and she definitely does the same for me. I'm constantly asking myself if there's something I can do that'll make her smile, or make her happy, or make a facet of her life easier. It's not wasting time when you're doing something for your ride-or-die. I love her, and doing things just because it might make her smile is the whole point. This is something I've really struggled with in the past, but I'm starting to see it, and I'm starting to get it.

A BRIEF HISTORY OF TRYING

King Henry VIII wanted to annul his first marriage but the pope wouldn't let him so K.Hen created the Church of England and named himself the head of it—that way he could do whatever the hell he wanted. He ended up getting married six times, and two of those wives were beheaded. So, yeah, he was kind of a dick.

I THINK BACK to the romantic gestures of my childhood, and to the young dweeb who tried to sweep his classmates off their feet. The whole time, I was really looking for shortcuts. Again and again in dating I haven't wanted to put in the hard work. Romance isn't all flowers and vacations and meeting at the top of the Empire State Building and running to find her on New Year's Eve. It isn't bursting through the chapel doors to object to her marriage to the wrong man. It isn't being an insomniac in Seattle. It was none of those things I saw in the movies that populated my childhood, and it definitely wasn't whatever creepy Valentine's Day stalker packages I tried pulling. No, it's just choosing to put her before myself. It's the little things. The hard things. It's a million little "unromantic" gestures. It's learning how to share your life with another person and doing everything in your power to make them happy. And then maybe once in a while you surprise them with a cruise to Ibiza.

I needed to take that crucial next step forward as a boyfriend but I lacked the tools. I think back to my fears of moving in together, my anxieties of not being ready for marriage or having children . . . of not being the man she deserves. But ultimately, it just requires dedication and belief. Dedication to her—putting her needs before my own and loving her always through ups and downs, when I'm being stupid and the (very) rare occasions when she's wrong. And belief—belief that I am valid, that I'm worthy of being loved, and that there's a reason she's with me to begin with, that it's not just some mistake. Meeting Maggie was, I repeat, the greatest thing that's ever happened to me.

Let her know it every day, and don't fuck this up, kid.

WHAT WE LEARNED

* Dating is all about confidence. Don't think too much. Don't spent more than fifteen seconds crafting a text message. Prepare to be shot down and then brush it all off.

* You never know when you're going to meet the One. Love finds you at the most unsuspecting moments, and sometimes in a gay bar bathroom.

* It's okay to go to bed angry with your siggy-oth—as long as you talk it out the next day.

* Date night is a simple and easy tradition to always make sure you are taking stock of your relationship. So are date lunches!

* Relationships are about respect, compromise, and selflessness. If you can master that, you never have to watch a cheesy romcom again. (Don't have to, but still can, because they're delightful!)

CHAPTER SIX

Family

They say friends are the new family. I mean, we're not sure who "they" is but they sound pretty reliable. For us, the labels *friend*, *family member*, and *coworker* get all jumbled up and basically mean the same thing. But what about our *actual* families? You know, those who raised us? Remember those people?

The four of us have all been guilty at times of not being the best brother or son. We're really busy and there's *so much* Netflix to watch. Plus we get complacent. It's almost like the closer the bond with someone, the easier it is not to check in regularly. It's not like your mom is going to disown you. Probably. So we want to look at the . . . let's call them *complicated* . . . relationships we have with our families, how we let them down, how they let us down, how all of that reflects poorly on us, and what we can do about it. We're regretting this already.

What's Wrong with Us

WHILE THE OTHER GUYS surely have domestic problems of their own, I'm the only one with the literal papers to prove it. My parents were immigrants and I grew up in a town where no one looked like me. Check. I'm a child of a divorce from a home that broke up and scattered across the globe. Check. I hate unwarranted hugs. Triple check. You could not write a better backstory for a character with a simmering suspicion of affection.

I have always had a hard time expressing my truths to my family. My parents didn't hug me every night—instead they conditioned me with values of achievement through diligence and action. Rather than coddling my dreams, they made me prove that I had the mettle to successfully reach my goals. Say what you want about Asian Americans or families from similar cultural backgrounds: we get shit done, and the one thing we sacrifice is emotionally opening ourselves up. Yes, my family and I love one another, but our particular way of showing it smacked of the formality one would associate with colleagues in a business setting. We were Korean, Texan, conservative, Christian, and desperately trying to fit in.

In hindsight, my parents raised us this way to not only survive our surroundings, but also to progress far beyond them, and it worked. My sisters and I are at the top of our respective fields—and if happiness were truly defined by success, then we should be leading blissfully jubilant existences. This, as we all know, is never the case, and although the foundation on which we constructed our social personas was made up of cold, hard, impressive steel, it doesn't erase the hot, fiery, emotional furnace that burns within each of us.

My family and the generations before them, because of this instinctive need to, first and foremost, stay alive, were never taught or allowed to channel the warm, desperate need for sentimental validation. And so when I came into this world, feelings ablaze, an unmanageable artistic force—I was pressured to keep it all under wraps. I tried to lock it up in a small, concrete box in the center of my heart, without instructions on how to properly allow others to take a peek inside.

I was an adult beyond my years in so many areas: school, self-reliance, intelligence, aptitude—but like so many kids whose family's focus was on career over playtime, I was woefully unprepared and infantile when it came to making friends. It wasn't until I broke that concrete box in my heart and allowed my passion and sensitivity to flow through my work that

I started to manage my relationships in a more healthy, controlled manner—but what's left is that hole.

Many of us carry around that gaping empty space where the box used to reside, and as charismatic and well adjusted as I may appear in videos or in person today, I continue to be wary of the people who enter my orbit. Hell, I'm even heedful of my own flesh and blood—I am a product of divorce, after all. Siblings fight. Marriages fall apart. Families are bound by an imaginary idea—blood. So I am going to try to close the gap between me and my family in a way I've never attempted. I'm going to allow myself to be intimate and sentimental and open through the help of my friends. This is going to be an absolute nightmare.

WE DON'T TALK a lot about our families in The Try Guys. That's partly because it doesn't come up a ton in the content of our videos, and partly because it's not our right to talk publicly about our family members' lives (yes, I am aware of the irony that we're about to do just that). The fatherhood series is the most we've spoken about our families, since our dads were a part of those videos. One of the biggest revelations in that video is that my family doesn't say "I love you" to each other. It's something I always wondered about but never thought to ask my dad until then. He said it simply came from not wanting to embarrass my

brothers and me, and it just sort of stuck. Which I suppose I can accept.

My whole family is independent. My two brothers and I all live across the country from each other, pursuing our own lives and goals. I don't talk to my parents a ton. I used to chat with them on the phone roughly every other month, while Becky and her parents talk on the phone almost every day. Only recently have I begun chatting with my mom somewhat daily. However, it's literally Facebook chat, and they are only short exchanges of "Hi, what's new, not much, bye!" but I like that it gives us a lower-touch way to communicate. We're all busy people living our own exciting lives, and we still care about one another, but this is how we exist as a family.

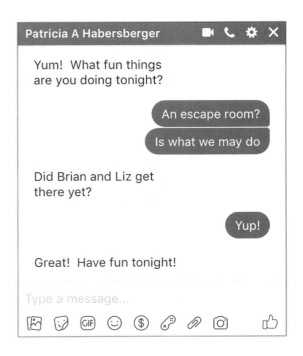

But I feel like I should challenge this notion. So far, what I have learned from writing this book is that our habits and preferences are just what's comfortable, but that ultimately you choose what your habits are and what "comfortable" really means. Just because my family and I have never really kept in touch that much, it doesn't mean it has to be that way forever.

SOME OF MY FRIENDS talk about not showing or vocalizing affection with their families, which I find insane. Not because I'm judging, but just because it's just so foreign to my family's dynamic. We hug, we kiss, we share blankets on the couch, and we definitely say "I love you," oftentimes as a corollary for saying good-bye. My parents, ever the supportive pair, are also probably the two most dedicated Try Guys fans on the planet (with apologies to everyone else). My sister and I don't fight. My cat ruled the house with a commanding but gentle fist. We were a tight-knit and loving unit, just teetering on the edge of nauseatingly cute. They all put up with a ton of bullshit raising me, all with a smile, and believe me when I say I was not an easy kid to raise.

Throughout the years, my parents have encouraged a few of my admittedly insane life and career choices. There wasn't even much of a hesitation when I started doing some of the more . . . let's say "out there" on-camera antics. One of my first YouTube appearances involved tattooing a smiley face on my ass, filmed for millions of people to see. People always ask if it's real—yes, it's real, and yes, it's still hilarious. I feared a huge lecture, but was met with more of an eye-roll. My

parents are cool, and they respected me and my sister enough not to micromanage and to let us make our own decisions, er, mistakes. Throughout childhood, instead of telling me that I should stop filming my toys and focus on some real hobbies, my parents helped me double down on being a total goof with after-school activities aimed at feeding my creativity and alternative pastimes. They didn't just help shape me, they totally enabled me—in a good way.

My younger sister Stephanie and I, incongruent to the basic fundamentals of siblinghood, have always been close and we seldom fought. It's not a stretch to say she's my best friend. She was my first audience, and I made it my job throughout childhood to make her laugh. I'm not talking cheap gags like making fart noises with my hands. No, this was highbrow stuff, like—get this—putting a pillow over my head and bumbling around the room, knocking into things. Mr. Pillow Head crushed every time.

My mother, in a stroke of genius, was able to preemptively extinguish any sibling rivalry, jealousy, or possessiveness by turning every-

THE HIDDEN POWER OF F*CKING UP

A BRIEF HISTORY OF TRYING

On one hand, Liam and Noel Gallagher of the band Oasis fucking *hate* each other. They have been ripping into each other in the press (and to each other's faces) since the early 1990s and have reportedly brawled on multiple occasions. On the other hand: "Wonderwall."

thing into a game. She told me that my new baby sister was going to try to steal all my toys, and that I could trick her by pretending to be into something super useless. As a result, anytime Stephi got grabby, it turned into a joke instead of a fight. That's some next-level-parenting ninja shit there. If you get one thing out of this chapter, let it be this: trick your children into not fighting by being smarter than them.

I've only recently come to recognize how much of a role my family played in shaping who I am, and I can't say I've done enough as an adult to properly thank them. Hearing the other guys talk got me thinking, and I imagine some of you out there are like me—you say "I love you" out of muscle memory instead of feeling the weight of the words. The impact my family has had on my life has been profound, and as I've grown older I've slipped into periods of being distant, of not calling as often as I should, and of not expressing how much they mean to me. It's something I need to rectify, especially now that we're all adults, because time is precious and I want all my future "I love you's" to be impactful and sincere.

Meet Wesley

WHEN ARIEL AND I welcomed our first child, Wesley, into the world last year, let's just say we were *not* prepared. I don't think parents are ever truly ready, but because Wes arrived nearly a month early, we were *definitely* not ready. Ariel and I had been putting the boards on the beautiful new deck that her father had built (pretty much entirely by himself—the man's a machine). Throughout the day, she occasionally complained of cramps and as the afternoon wore on she started doing less drilling of screws and more organizing of tools. Then she took a long bath and went to bed early.

That evening, at midnight, she starting having contractions. For the first two hours she furiously googled "phantom labor pains" and downloaded an app to time the contractions. Around 2 a.m. she woke me up to say, "Uh . . . I think I might be going into labor."

That was the last thing I was thinking. Since it was nearly *a month* before her due date, I thought I could give her a shoulder rub and we would both go back to bed. But the contractions seemed to be getting worse. Finally Ariel suggested we go to the hospital. We were so woefully unprepared that we had to print out a packing list from a doula website in order to figure out what to bring. We hadn't even picked out a name for our baby!

I drove carefully to the hospital, thinking the last thing I needed was a 3 a.m. Saturday collision with a drunk driver. I even pulled over to the side of the road a few times so that Ariel could bear out a contraction.

We were checked in and the nurse wouldn't let Ariel eat or drink anything because of a potential emergency C-section. She checked Ariel's dilation: 4.5 centimeters already. I'll never forget when the nurse said, "Oh honey, you're staying with us tonight!"

We moved from triage to the labor and delivery area, where it was much more comfortable and where there was even a couch "for Dad." I was "Dad" everywhere we went. Initially I kept thinking, "I'm a person and my name is Ned." But that night, "Dad" it was. I quickly grew to love it.

Soon it seemed like the tension of an emergency had been defused. Ariel was allowed to eat and drink again and they set up a nitrous oxide tank to help with the labor pains, which was Ariel's preferred pain management technique. That's when I watched the nurse set up a table containing what looked like *one thousand tiny knives*. In reality, it was a delivery table with a dense array of tiny scalpels, scissors, gauze, and paper towels, but in my sleep-deprived state I thought it was a harbinger of death. With Ariel lying back and nitrous flowing calmly into her lungs, I stared at this shiny, shiny table.

The labor went on. And on. And on. Throughout the morning, we tried different labor positions: On her side with a squishy ball between her legs. Facing backward and gripping the edge of the bed. Bouncing on a ball. Standing up and leaning on me. Leaning over the bed. Despite our exhaustion and her pain, we laughed and held each other. We must have played the entire Ed Sheeran discography about three times. After twelve hours of labor, her water still hadn't broken.

The doctor finally arrived and got to work. She slipped a little plastic stick inside Ariel and *pop*, water was suddenly pouring out of her. It was a puddle about an inch deep (sorry, reader, these are things you need to know, eventually). After that, the pain really intensified. On a scale from 1 to 10, every contraction was a 12. Every five minutes, the whir of the nitrous machine started as Ariel breathed in and then she started yelling out, gripping the hospital bed, holding my hand. And she was still not dilated enough to push.

Another half hour went by. Then it was time. The room transformed into a delivery suite. The ceiling opened up and a big surgical light craned down. The sheet got whipped off the table with all the tiny knives. The doctor suited up in a mask, gloves, and smock. She counted each piece of gauze so that none got left inside. Each contraction, the nurses asked Ariel to push. It was excruciating. She was straining so hard. I could not bear to see her in pain. But she's so strong. The doctor, nurses, and our doula were superhelpful,

coaching Ariel through each push and encouraging her to rest in between. I was holding her hands with an iron grip and supporting her head.

I have never seen someone exert themselves so completely in my life. I will forever be inspired by her strength. Her entire body and face would contort and strain to *push* that baby out. She was dripping with sweat, taking one deep breath and then pure exertion for ten seconds. It lasted for six or seven contractions, about half an hour. They showed me the baby's head starting to peek through. I was so on edge that I saw a single drop of blood and the overlapping head bones and thought for sure it was all going wrong.

Then, all of a sudden, *plop*. The baby came out all at once and they pulled him up to Ariel's chest, skin to skin. He let out a deafening cry. The three of us held each other for a long time. It was amazing. It was beautiful. Finally we got to meet Wesley James Fulmer—Wes because it sounded nice and James after my father.

Eugene Tries to Get Close to His Family . . . with a Little Help from His Friends!

IN THE EARLY 2017 VIDEO "The Try Guys Take a Lie Detector Test," Zach asks me point-blank, "Do you know how much we care about you?" I reply with a tense "No." The machine says I'm telling the truth, and Keith remarks, "We've gotta be better about that."

That's the grand symbolic point I'm starting from: I'm the guy who feels neither pain nor empathy, who neither consoles nor is consoled. Whose relationship with his family can best be described as "arm's-length." And who doesn't even think his best friends care about him. But what I'm going to do now is give those friends free rein in helping me actually connect with my family.

My entire family is coming to town for my grandmother's ninetieth birthday. A perfect opportunity for me to—shudder—spend intimate time with them. But it's up to the Try Guys to assign me the tasks I must accomplish with the ten—yes, ten—family members who are descending upon Los Angeles for this reunion.

The guys take turns meeting with me in the Try Guys' offices and I'm riddled

with anxiety. Keith is up first. I've always been somewhat envious of Keith's perma-plastered smile and his innate ability to make anyone around him feel like they've been friends since diapers. To become known for being a joyous person is unfathomable for me, and Keith has managed to do so with gusto.

He sits down in front of me like the Cheshire Cat. I'm suddenly filled with the deepest dread that he'll require me to plaster a toothy grin across my face during my family reunion, which is a hell I don't think I would be physiologically able to recover from. Instead, he riddles me this:

 Eugene, this is what I want you to do with your family. You have to give each and every person a compliment. Something they haven't heard you tell them before, and it has to be nice, and it should make them feel good.

"NO," I RECOILED, the word flying from my mouth before I could swallow it. Compliments, weirdly enough, fall plainly into a category of topics I generally avoid like the plague. As someone who admittedly receives plenty of compliments online, I abhor the feelings they give me because I feel as if they come from a disingenuous place. Constructive criticism? Clever insults? Real talk? Now you're speaking my language. But compliments? Sugary frosting without a cake, in my book.

Keith knows this, and I hate him in the moment for suggesting this. The fact remains that I can't just say something cute about my aunt's scarf and let that be that; no, I must be like Keith and be serious in my niceties. I must make them *believe.*

Zach is next, and I hope upon hope that he doesn't give me something as difficult as Keith has. I relate to Zach. He's known for being a soft, bratty, totally incapable character in our cast dynamic, but as a fully realized person he's actually quite biting in wit and assured in mental dexterity. He recognizes moments when I'm crippled by emotional issues because I know he's had some version of it himself in his childhood.

He sits down in front of me and just from the glint in his eyes, I immediately can see the direction he's going to head in. Although our communities are very different, his Jewish upbringing gives him some insight into more closed-off, achievement-oriented families who value tradition, and his task for me feels derived from that background:

 I want you to get each of your family members to tell you a secret. Something that you don't know about them yet. Something they wouldn't tell you unless you ask.

WELL, FUCK—as if I thought complimenting people would be hard enough, I'm now going to have to demand sincere action out of others, which is nearly impossible in a secretive, out-of-sight, out-of-mind family like mine. If someone like my grandmother has gone almost an entire century without telling a single soul something personal (and trust me, people have asked), how in the hell would she ever entrust that bit of information to her wild, eccentric grandson?

I wonder, with someone like Zach and his family, who operate in a more communicative, warm manner, if constantly asking about what's going on in each other's lives has in fact brought them closer over the years. I see the way he communicates with his parents and sister and I recognize something familiar and something foreign: they playfully jab, which I completely understand, but I'm lost when I see how involved they expressly want to be in one another's lives. Although we're all doing relatively well, my sisters and parents and I are living parallel lives, rarely crossing each other's paths for the occasional holiday, with check-ins over texting or email about what's happening in our careers. We have gone months without speaking to one another. And now I'm going to have to seek out their secrets.

Finally, Ned enters the room, and every fiber of my being immediately tenses up. While Keith inspires me and Zach provokes me, Ned simply horrifies me as both a friend and an organism that breathes, thinks, and worst yet—loves openly. I mean gushily, unabashedly loves, so overbearingly so that his actual brand as an entertainer Venn-diagrams winsomely with his roles as a husband and father. I would be lying if I said I've never thrown up in my mouth just the tiniest bit when he gazes longingly into his wife's eyes and whispers sweet nothings. Ned's nuclear family is like a Norman Rockwell painting, perpetually gathered around some vision of a dinner table, basking in each other's affection. Although I'm sure much of what I write sounds like a thinly veiled slight, I assure you that it's more of a foreigner's observation of something powerfully, unbreakably domestic, and I gaze upon their portrait in the museum as if it's a piece of abstract art. Ned sits down and says to me:

 Eugene, you have to hug them. All of them. Not a quick hug, not a pat on the back. A real, strong, loving hug.

KRYPTONITE. Ned knew it, and he threw it at my face, and he did so with a coy, shit-eating grin. Sure, there's a lot of negative things swirling around menacingly within me, but externally, the one thing that will surely invoke my fight-or-flight reflex is when someone comes in for a hug. Something as simple as a hug was not regularly exercised as part of my family's physical vocabulary. I didn't willingly give my older sister a hug until we were both in college—my dad and I took even longer to get to that point. I can say with confidence that out of the ten relatives I'm seeing at our reunion, I had really only hugged half of them. Even when The Try Guys try to hug me, I recoil, and I work with them 24/7.

All three of my best friends knew that if I were to take on a truly Herculean try with my family, I would have to face my issues with closeness head-on, and to further bolster our friendship I would have to listen to and trust in their challenges without question. You remember the trust falls you used to do at camp? It felt akin to that, only my buddies were pushing me, hard, out into space over the heads of ten people who had no idea that I was falling down toward them. Would they catch me?

Friends show their love in times of trouble,
not in happiness.

—*Fucking Euripides*

The Three Women Who Shaped Me

THERE ARE THREE WOMEN who shaped me. One taught me to express myself, one taught me to laugh, and one taught me to work my ass off. Sing that last sentence to the tune of Ariana Grande's "Thank U, Next" for maximum results.

It begins with Grandma (not to be confused with Grammy, my other grandmother, whom we'll get to shortly). Evelyn Kornfeld (formerly Evelyn Wahrhaftig—can't see why they changed that name at Ellis Island) was born in Berlin in 1933. Not the best time and place to be a Jew. Her father, a mainstay of the Berlin theater scene, saw the warning signs and had the foresight to leave. He first found a new home in Copenhagen and sent for the family, then they later fled to America when Denmark was no longer a safe option. They left everything—their home, their careers, their friends—and started anew without a penny to their name. Without that risk, I wouldn't be here today.

My grandmother passed away a few years back, and one of my biggest regrets in life is not taking the time to learn about her past, to hear stories from an exceptional life. When I was a kid, I remember feeling afraid to ask, that it would be awkward and out of line. Or maybe I was just more interested in myself. I didn't take full advantage of the time we had together, and I'll never be able to get that back.

Grandma played a pivotal role in shaping my identity, and she did so likely without realizing the impact it would have. When we cleared out her apartment, I found an unassuming composition notebook in the back of the drawer previously reserved for my toys. The moment my fingers touched it, I knew what was inside. For years, every time I went to see Grandma I would invent new stories—some inspired by our day of visiting the Bronx Zoo or climbing rocks in the park, others from the deep recesses of my imagination. As I sat dictating my stories, Grandma transcribed them, word for word, improper syntax and all. After all these years, she kept the notebook. She kept every story I ever wrote.

Thanks to her, I have that piece of history, and through it, a memory of the bond we shared. Inside the pages of those notebooks are stories that run the gamut from thrilling tales about three fish with different patterns, to robbers hiding in the corner of a computer screen (huh?), to a time-traveling adventure involving bubble gum and a thunderstorm. The notebook ranges with stories from ages two(!) to six. But between the lines is a snapshot of the experiences we shared—the day trips, the museums, the laughter—and the ways in which she expressed her love to me.

Grandma was the first person to recognize my love of storytelling, or at least the first not to tell me to shut up about it. The simplest act of love and kindness—listening to a kid who wanted so desperately to tell stories and entertain—set the events of my life into motion. She encouraged my stories, she enabled me to write them, and she kept them for me so that I would never lose the times we shared

together. For her it may have been the smallest of things—a fun activity to fill an afternoon. But for me it has meant the world. I never got to tell her in life, but here's hoping she knows.

If Grandma enabled my desire to tell stories, it was my other grandmother, *Grammy*, who dialed up my lovable goof side. Grammy showed me that grown-ups don't have to be "grown up," that it's possible to maintain a sense of childlike wonder and zeal even into your sixties and beyond. Our favorite game was crawling under the table at family dinners and tying people's shoelaces together. Her idea, I swear. It got old real fast for everyone involved except for us. Throughout my childhood, our interactions encouraged a certain appreciation for absurdity and finding the humor in everything. That mind-set follows me today and helped me forward in the darkest times of my life—appreciating that life is better when you're laughing, and that everything is funny if you look hard enough.

In fact—oh my God—I'm just realizing as I write this that my love of smiley faces comes from her. She's the reason I got that tattoo on my butt! It's a reminder to always smile and not take life so seriously. However, Grammy does not see it the same way and is still in complete denial about the whole thing. She's somehow convinced herself that it's not a tattoo at all and rather was drawn in Sharpie for the video. She politely refuses to hear any explanation of how that makes no sense and would very much like to change the subject now.

And finally, my mother, Margo, by far the strongest person I've ever met. She has the most robust work ethic in the known universe, and instilled in me a (borderline insane) drive to work harder and always keep pushing. She never stops moving and never gives up. When I hated my teacher in first grade and refused to learn how to read (seriously, Ms. Pugni was a real piece of shit and I stand by it), my mom made it her job to get me excited about books by reading the first Harry Potter aloud to me. She then refused to read the second book and said if I wanted to know what happened I'd have to learn to read myself. She won. She always won.

When I was in high school my mom was diagnosed with breast cancer and had to go through intense rounds of chemotherapy. Despite our protests, she sent me and my sister away for a month so that we'd miss the most trying period of her struggle. She didn't want us to see her at her low point. My memories of her are only of a strong, totally in-control badass. Before I knew it, she was back exercising every morning. She's now completely in remission, which should come as no surprise because cancer never stood a goddamn chance against her.

Over the years whenever I had moments of doubt, or worse, when laziness and complacency would rear its repulsive head, my mother was always there to give me a firm kick in the ass. As long as I can remember, my plan in life was to move out to Los Angeles and take a stab at Hollywood. After graduating, I moved back in with my parents, spending my days with friends in Brooklyn. I fell in love with the city and with the people. (Actually two different girls told me my glasses were cute and I was like, "Oh shit, I'm staying here forever.") My mom swept in and saw immediately that I really just wanted to putz around getting high and attend five-dollar concerts without ever bothering to find a real job. Instead of allowing for an argument, she opted for a more sensible approach. She sold my bed and (lovingly) kicked me out of the house. "You don't have a bed anymore, but Dad and I did get you a one-way ticket to Los Angeles." I moved in with Grammy in LA until I found my own place and got a job. I never looked back.

Meet the Family

TEN FAMILY MEMBERS. One weekend. Three challenges devised by my friends. Through the Try Guys' patented approach to new experiences, I've overcome the fear of embarrassing myself in front of millions of people. However, during my decades of time on this planet, I have yet to triumph over the crippling anxiety that comes with growing closer to my own family. Think that sounds like a stretch? Why don't we meet the players in this board game—but just remember that each party wields a wrench or a rope or a candlestick and isn't afraid to use it, genealogy be damned.

For the sake of protecting my already very private family (who I assure you will be far from thrilled when they find out I wrote about them in this book)*, I'm going to use numbers in place of their names. I have listed them in ascending order from who I already feel closest to—No. 1, all the way up to who I feel the most distance from—No. 10.

No. 1: my younger sister, whom I've always been very close to. Do you have a little sibling who's the princess of the roost? That's her, only this princess will casually slit your throat, walk over your remains, and not even bat an eyelash in order to achieve her set goals. Logical to a fault, unfathomably self-sufficient, and the shining example of what near perfection looks like in our family. I used to call her the "robot" because her operating systems were so smooth and malfunctioned only on the rarest of occasions, when she couldn't complete a checklist. Yes, in conclusion, the princess-angel-baby of our family is an android who will kill you if you get in her way.

No. 2: my older sister, whom I've also been very tight with, but only after college. We fought a lot as kids, and for good reason: while my little sister managed her concrete heart box with reasonable jurisdiction, my older sister and I retaliated against our feelings in dramatic, explosive ways. Once when we were kids, my sister kept telling me that I was, in fact, dead, and was a dumb-ass ghost who didn't

---

* From this point on, all of Eugene's family photos will be obscured to respect their privacy (and add to their mystery).

realize he was dead. My mother, rolling her eyes, told me to tell her that she was a liar, and several minutes later I came back crying even harder because my sister then told me that she would kill herself so that she could become a spirit and then murder me in the ghost world, and started chasing me with a kitchen knife. This was one of our nice fights.

We get along famously now, and although she has a high-powered job, beautiful home, indecorous sense of humor, and a chill husband, she draws the line at children. Both of my sisters, to drive a point home about my family, find the idea of having kids to be unnecessary, wasteful, and just plain gross—and if you feel compelled to do that thing where your voice gets higher and you plead, "But like that's what every woman says until they have kids," my sisters will laugh at you, find the nearest child, and punch it in the head to prove their point.

No. 3: this person lives far away and we have a very tight bond, but so much of her life is carefully hidden from me, both because of the distance and due to the fact that she feels pressured to constantly conceal her own true feelings.

Eventually we will get to No. 10: this person is going to be the hardest nut to crack. He is an enigma, difficult to speak with even in passing, and absolutely disinterested in getting to know what's happening in other people's lives. All three challenges I must achieve feel like they'll fall on deaf ears with No. 10.

Although I could fill volumes of therapy journals about my family's psychological history, this is an effort toward a better future, not a dwelling on an incongruous past, and I couldn't have conceived of a more opportune time than my grandmother's ninetieth birthday soirée. Since she lives in Los Angeles and most of the other party guests were travelers from out of town, I found myself volunteering for a position that I typically never enjoy: I oversaw and coordinated our entire itinerary.

Yes, unknowingly, I accidentally became a slightly more responsible brother/son/nephew because of this book's challenge, because I had to put work into organizing ten (thirteen, if you count accompanying non-Korean husbands and boyfriends) people arriving from different states and countries with hotels all over town. Lord knows you do not want to experience the hell that is explaining rideshare apps to people who just discovered how to text properly.

My sisters, who stayed at my apartment during the festivities, both examined me in the backhanded way we appraise one another as siblings and commented, "Well, it's really nice that you're trying to put everyone's affairs in order, but don't fuck things up like you usually do." I responded with a spiteful, "Thanks so much— you look skinnier than you did last time, thank God."

The rest of my family arrived in Los Angeles a few days before the big birthday weekend. I sent texts and emails and phone calls to keep everyone apprised of each other's whereabouts, and as the sun rose on the first official morning everyone was finally within a five-mile radius of one another. Without having even seen them, I already felt exhausted by how much I had to converse with them. Already stressed from my own work and life responsibilities, I reminded myself that I'll go to jail if I murder my own family—then who would feed my dogs? I got in my car, my sisters loudly in tow, and headed to the mall.

There are certain strategic benefits to a large, outdoor California shopping center for a family that has a weakness for retail and the sensual siren song of slashed prices. For Keith's compliment challenge, I can split up the group with little to no effort and pick them off, one by one like in a horror movie. There's the added perk that as I say the nicest thing to each of them, the others, like innocent deer in the woods, won't be tipped off by my devious game and dart away from my admiration rifle. Even as I write this I know I'm spouting remarkably maniacal nonsense for someone aiming to get closer to their family, but as we strolled past the artisanal ice-cream stands and luxury luggage, I felt most comfortable imagining my quest as a dangerous, sexy game, one in which my victims were totally unaware that I was about to spring some serious sweetness on them.

I had a day to get these compliments out, because my grandma's birthday dinner was the following evening. After lunch, the herd predictably splintered into three groups: serial shoppers, casual browsers, and café sitters. Feeling spritely, I decide to accompany the first group through what was sure to be a rapid succession of clothing stores. We left the slower animals and entered AllSaints.

It's a unisex retailer, so seeing men's items, I immediately know I can corner No. 3 and take her out with a compliment pretty quickly because she's always itching to buy gifts for me. My face relaxes in that dead-eyed fashionista stare that my sisters and I have perfected over years of training—you know, the one where employees know not to bother you but also expect you might buy something based on how bored you look. No. 3 sees me rifling numbly through leather jackets and she immediately appears at my side and starts picking items that could look great for the fall.

It won't take long for you, the reader, to clearly figure out who No. 3 is, but she's probably the most special to me of everyone on the list, and maybe because of my yearning to be closest to her I chose to target her with my newfound niceness first. As she grabs what seems like the seventh sweater, I clear my throat, look her straight in the eyes, and say, "You look very beautiful."

She laughs quickly, brushing it off with the automatic modest "No, but thank you," and grabs another sweater. I pause, the realization dawning on me that this was a poor excuse for a sincere compliment. Saying nice things about someone's appearance, especially to a woman, and especially in my family, is common, cheap currency. Rich people do it. Men do it. Everyone does it. I feel my face run slightly hotter—am I the tiniest bit ashamed that my first go at it was so bourgeois and misinformed?

I really examine what she's doing. She pushes a few more items into the shopping cart that is my arms, and it suddenly strikes me what to say.

"You don't have to buy me anything."

"Nonsense, of course I do."

"I'm just really happy that I get to spend time with you, Mom."

She pauses for a moment, a faint glimmer of something powerful and bright in her eye, trapped at a fixed point, but shining through a polite, controlled gaze. I don't know how often I've actually said that sentence to her out loud, but I do know how much she treasures the few days a year we get to see one another.

She retorts, "Then why don't you visit me more often," and the moment's passed, but it's a keeper forever.

The Car Seat Test

LITTLE DID I KNOW that one of our most challenging moments as a family would come a mere forty-eight hours into Wesley's life. The few days after he was born were spent breastfeeding and getting to know the baby while still in the hospital. A stream of visitors and service providers were coming through our room seemingly at all hours of the day. We learned how to swaddle and how to feed. There were a slew of vision and hearing tests, exams, and shots. Then on the day that we were going to leave, he had his final test, something called the car seat test. Wes had to sit in a car seat in the hospital room for ninety minutes while hooked up to an oxygen and heartbeat monitor. It was designed to make sure that he had the strength to support his head for a long car trip in case we get stuck in traffic on the freeway.

I had already started loading up the car when, after sixty minutes, he failed the test. They whisked him off to the NICU in a tiny glass box. We were heartbroken, completely devastated. They ran a bunch of additional tests. He was hooked up to a tiny baby IV. He was crying and struggling. Recalling the memory of that day is very painful for me. It felt like there was nothing we could do. Right when we were getting ready to drive home, we had been sent to the worst place imaginable. Because Ariel was officially discharged, we had to switch to a courtesy room they had for us, but there was no cot or second pillow, so the two of us just lay in a single hospital bed together, and cried.

The NICU is a scary place. Fortunately, the nurses, doctors, and administrators who worked there were a tireless, comforting presence. We tried to focus on the positives: Wes was healthy and just needed more time to grow. With two extra days of 24/7 nursing support, Ariel learned how to pump and we finally got more than five hours of sleep. We were lucky. After forty-eight hours, Wes took the car seat test again. For ninety minutes straight, we kept an anxious vigil. Would his oxygen levels start dropping again? Fortunately he slept the whole time and passed the test! We finally brought him home to start our new life together, excited for the future.

Since then, it has been an indescribable feeling watching Wes grow and experience the world. I've gained this intimate microcosmic perspective on how a tiny human explores the world. He starts to realize that he has hands. Then he finds out he can grab things. Then he discovers he can roll over back and forth. As I write this he is just in the very early stages of crawling and can slowly swivel himself around the floor to grab a toy to play with. So cute!

But this isn't just a book about how adorable Wes is; it's about how to overcome your challenges. So let me share just a few of the obstacles thrown my way during fatherhood, and how I was able to (somewhat) successfully navigate them.

The number one hurdle is no sleep. For the first three, four, even six months or longer, we woke up multiple times a night to care for the baby. No matter how much sleep you think you need, I guarantee you that the introduction of a newborn will disrupt it. Before the baby, I would try to get seven to eight hours of sleep. After the baby, I was lucky if I got five, and it was usually sporadic and interrupted. After several weeks of sleep deprivation, it started to take a toll on all aspects of my life. It was harder to focus on simple tasks, I was more irritable, and I started to enjoy even the good things less. And if what I know from spy movies is accurate, extreme sleep deprivation is actu-

ally a form of torture. The savior to this was Ariel. By trading off nights, we each allowed the other person that necessary time to let their body recover.

The second biggest challenge for me was dealing with feelings of guilt. As a new father, I was constantly feeling guilty that I wasn't doing enough. There seemed to be not enough hours in the day to have a job, have a relationship, and give a child all of the physical, mental, and emotional nourishment that he needs. Honestly, just caring for a child alone would take 100 percent of the time. So I'm very thankful that I was able to take several weeks off from work, and that the other Try Guys picked up the slack so I could be completely present with Ariel and Wesley. I think we should encourage all employers to give plenty of time—paid time—for new parents to bond with their kids.

There's also so much judgment you receive as a new parent. It could be a stranger on the street who wants to give you unsolicited advice, or it could be friends, parents, or in-laws. It could even come from Ariel. Especially Ariel. After all, she's the one other person just as invested in the baby as I am. Anytime you get judged, it makes you feel both defensive about your own point of view and guilty about actually having made a mistake. The only way past it is to check your ego and remember that everyone is just trying to help. And when you inevitably do mess up, give yourself a break. Remind yourself that just trying your best is enough. There's always more you could be doing or something different you could be doing, but if you're doing the best you can, there's nothing to be guilty about. That said, Ariel *is* usually right, so I try to do things her way when possible.

The third challenge has been fear. Fear that my baby is going to hurt himself, fear that he's not growing up fast enough (or slow enough). The number of times that I have gently placed my hand on his chest to make sure that he's still breathing is . . . a lot. I remember a moment when I was first driving Wes home from the hospital, where we stopped to get gas, and all of a sudden, I saw even the simple act of going to a gas station in a totally different light. The fumes of the gas, could those hurt Wesley's brain? The other cars going through the parking lot, what if they hit our car? That man over there, is he getting too close? We've definitely already had our first "false alarm" trip to the emergency room after a tiny head bonk, where the doctor so sweetly told us, "This is not an emergency situation."

Throughout all these challenges, my family has pitched in to help in such a comforting and supportive way. We have been so fortunate to have a steady stream of grandparents coming to stay with us to help out. My mom loves reading to Wes in the mornings. My dad is a pro at goofy peekaboo playtime. Auntie Grace and Auntie Danielle are on speed dial for babysitting. I've developed a deeper respect and appreciation for my in-laws, whether it's Ariel's dad building us a fence *and a deck* or Ariel's mom rocking Wes to sleep. And through it all is the beautiful mother of my child, who I know is facing the same challenges but never lets it show: my love, Ariel. Yes, of course there are challenges to raising a newborn baby, but the experience has brought my family closer to me than ever before. I know that Wes is going to grow up in an environment bursting with love, and that makes me beam with joy.

Fishing for Compliments

UGH, we're STILL shopping.

After having my sweet but brief moment with Mom, we all move on to Compartes, a gourmet chocolatier in the mall. I find a seamless segue in with No. 4, who I recall having a notorious sweet tooth. She's cool and we've always gotten along, but we haven't spent a lot of time together, so I don't know much beyond the basics of her life.

I point out one especially gluttonous-looking candy bar and mention how much she must be desiring a bite.

"Actually, I don't really eat that much candy anymore," she informs me, while picking it up to read the ingredients. "Fuck," I think. I can't even get past rudimentary knowledge of some of my family members with this first compliments round. My mind scrambles and I reflexively respond: "Well, you could eat all the sugar you want because you've always managed to stay so skinny!"

"Thanks!" she flippantly replies. Double fuck. It dawns on me that, like with my mom, I have fallen back onto hollow physical commendations in place of meaningful praise.

While Sisters 1 and 2 browse alongside us, I sense a new direction to get to payday. I nod toward them and say to No. 4, "Well, I've always liked you way better than Numbers One and Two because, you know, we get one another."

No. 4 grins, almost proudly, before agreeing enthusiastically. "Yeah, we're just way more chill."

Nowhere in the rules did it say that I wasn't allowed to put down one family member in order to nail a compliment with another. Call it a loophole if you must; with that small but validating victory I turned my attention to the toughest customers of all . . . the people I'm closest to . . . my sisters.

Surely, you would think, compliments would come most easily for those you are the most communicative with, but to witness the way in which my sisters and I casually chat is akin to a teen drama where everyone is the mean blond girl. In this sisterhood, you'd be torn apart for showing such silly signs of weakness.

Needless to say, I found myself on the verge of anxiety as the serial shoppers made their way to Nordstrom to spend what was sure to be an eternity trying on shoes. I knew this would be the perfect time to ensnare them—they can't run away from me while encumbered by stilettos. As we scanned the racks, I searched the inner depths of my mind for benevolence.

I decide to go for the slightly less ferocious of the sisters—No. 1, the younger tiger shark, who lurks patiently on a bench as a salesperson grabs the correct size of heels in the back.

I sit next to her, trying to decipher exactly what my way in is, and ask, "How's work? Still considering quitting?" Without going into much private detail, she had entrusted me with the information that a major occupational change was afoot, one that would be both momentous and a scary leap into the unknown. She lights up, prepared for her turn to share, and as she slides on a pair of suede peep-toe pumps she dives into the prospects of her potential career pivot. I simply need to be a better listener and give her the comfortable space to spill her guts. When she finishes her impassioned speech, she looks at me with a rare need for some form of verbal validation.

"I'm very proud of you," I say. "I think you're going to be totally kick-ass, whatever decision you make." This was high, honest praise; even the word "proud" was not a sentiment we'd toss around haphazardly. She smiles, agreeing with my assessment, and decides to try on another pair of shoes.

I could tell that I had succeeded in giving No. 1 an earnest compliment, but now I had to set my sights on a more discriminating target: the elder, great white shark, who was slipping on a couple of different versions of thigh-high winter boots.

No. 2 and I have developed an outstanding relationship after a childhood of searing, blind hatred—to say that neither of us processed our emotional issues healthily and redirected them at others would be an understatement. Now we lightly jab where we used to KO, and our humorous banter is a minefield to have to dig some sort of veneration from.

I decide to just go for it. "Those look great! Your legs look really long."

She examines her gams in the mirror. "Hmm, yes, well, I need it to cut at the thigh because I'm so petite."

I chuckle. "Yeah, you're pretty fucking tiny . . ."

Damn it, don't insult her, and stop talking about appearance.

She sits to try on another style, unfazed by what must have seemed like Yang-style small talk.

I cross my arms and take a shot in the dark. "You know, you've always been . . . so much smarter than me. I can be pretty stupid sometimes. Like, a real idiot."

Technically, this was a compliment—after all, Keith never said I couldn't re-route an insult toward thyself. No. 2 pauses, thinks this over, and huffs aloud. "Oh, that's not entirely true—you do possess a certain, how should I say, emotional intelligence that I don't. You're so . . . nice." She stands in her next pair of boots, taking a few test steps. "You are definitely an idiot, though."

I scoff, mildly surprised. "You think I'm nice?"

She shrugs, admiring her prospective buy. "I mean, none of us are really all that nice, but comparatively, if I'm smarter than you, then you're nicer than me. People tend to like you, but maybe that's because most people are also idiots." She rolls her eyes off my questioning stare. "You're welcome."

Then it creeps up on me, as we all reconvene at a coffee shop in the mall: I had hardly done more than make inroads with Nos. 1–4, those I'm already the most familiar with. But what about 5–10, those whom I didn't know well enough to deliver something truly meaningful? As I handed each of them their coffee, I took a stab.

To No. 6, with her Americano: "Your, uh, makeup has gotten better since I saw you last!" (What an inane, beauty-specific thing to blurt out.) She is a relative I've always known but never really gotten close to, although I feel like she'd like to be more involved if she could. She's got a dry sense of humor I've recently come to appreciate.

She takes it, chortling. "Oh, thank you, it's the exact same." Fail.

To No. 7, holding her water: "Are you having fun? I'm so excited to be here with you." (Nailed it, I hope.) No. 7 is extremely precious to me on paper, but in reality, I have barely engaged with her enough to feel like I know much about her experience beyond what other people have told me. She is of particular interest to me in this try.

She grimaces. "No, you are always so busy." She didn't even believe me.

To Nos. 8 and 9, with their cappuccinos: "You know, the others all agree that you are most definitely the most normal out of all of us!" (This was true, but also an alarmingly strange thing to point out.)

They smile politely. No. 9 remarks, "No, maybe you think that because you are always acting so crazy." They laugh. (Great, I simply made myself look more bizarre.)

To No. 10, with his soda—I literally had no idea what to throw out there, so I volleyed a trite "You look nice."

He sips his Coke and points at my ankles. "Why do you wear pants like that?" Fails all around.

No. 5, whom I gently hand a double espresso, would be my last stand. This person is a very impactful figure in my life, whom I respect, though he is someone I haven't had the chance to pry at emotionally. It's very difficult to get a word in edgewise in regular conversation, so he'll be a particular challenge because he's a terrible listener. I take the seat next to him.

He inquires about how my work is going, and I give him an abridged summary before he indulges me with a lengthy, analytical response. But this time, I really try to listen to him. His lecture, interestingly, expands from a commendation that he saw I was doing well and enjoyed watching my hard work pay off. This, in and of itself, was a casual but compassionate compliment toward me, and I find myself beaming.

It's easy to overlook others with creative dreams of their own when you're so rigidly pigeonholed as the artisan in your family—or whatever role you were proclaimed to play within your tree. I know No. 5 always had a deep knowledge and appreciation for the arts, but seldom had I connected that fervor with my own career, and even then I never would conclude that he would, in ways, substantially see some of himself in me. He is, after all, someone whose vocation involves more numbers than imagination, so I never considered him a cultural peer, even though as he bent my ear, it was abundantly clear that he was a maestro consumer of creative crafts.

A spontaneous inkling fills me and I point out, "You know, I think you would have been a fantastic artist. You definitely have the spirit of one."

He processes this, tilting his head. "Mmm, maybe, but it just wasn't the right time or place or . . . life for me, I think. We'll never know." He shows the whisper of a grin. "I think I would have been a good musician, yes."

Even for the most ephemeral of moments, I think I've reached him.

We leave the mall, the goodwill built from my 50 percent success rate nearly demolished by the nightmare that is organizing everyone's safe passage home to distant hotels. Failure, at this point, feels unavoidable. Because if I can barely bestow compliments correctly, how the hell am I going to get them to tell me a secret?

104 Years Young

THE PERSON IN MY FAMILY whom I feel most guilty about not calling enough is my grandpa, who is about to turn 104. Yeah, One Hundred and frickin' Four Years Old! Crazy, I know. He lives in an assisted living facility, and while the last six years I've been reaching out to him more than ever before, I still have only seen him three times. He's surprisingly aware for his age. He apparently has a girlfriend right now, which is beyond cute.

He's a short guy, having survived rickets as a kid. Despite that, he served in the military as an airplane engineer and then taught himself to be a chemist. He met my grandmother in Scotland when he was stationed there for World War II. She immigrated to America on a boat with war brides, as was apparently the case with many soldiers. He once told me that when she came over, all the other brides were wearing beautiful dresses and makeup, and my grandmother was wearing a brown trench coat, "looking almost like a military official herself." Nonetheless, they had a happy marriage and had a few kids living in the German district of Queens in New York City.

I wasn't always so disconnected from him. Before he turned one hundred, I did a little work to get to know him better. I brought a camera and filmed an hour-

or-so interview about his life and the military and Grandma. He talked a lot about how he felt it was important for couples to "have a hobby together." He and my grandma chose square dancing, and they became attached to it, dancing well into their eighties.

I regret not knowing my grandmother better; she died when I was in college. My dad would go on trips to see his parents, but we were all "too busy" to join him. That was certainly a mistake, but when you're young, you take a lot for granted. I've learned to forgive myself for lapses in judgment as a kid. It's only extra motivation for why I should be better now.

My other grandmother, Grandma McCarthy, made a savings account for my brothers and me to go to college with. She passed away when I was around ten, and I probably have never given enough thought and thankfulness to her for that gift. Knowing so many people now with student loans . . . I'm not sure if we would be where we are today without her.

Some of my family relationships have grown so much closer over time. For instance, my older brother Brian. We're great friends, but it wasn't always that way. Something about our personalities as kids really clashed. I think partly it came from Brian being the middle child and being exceptionally bright. As we grew up, I starting growing really fast. I think when I was six and he was ten we were about the same height. People thought we were twins and he really hated people thinking that there was any way a kid as smart and old as him could be confused with someone as young and goofy as me. Also, Brian really never wanted a lot of attention, while I was always making sure people paid attention to me—at whatever cost (see, well, the rest of the book).

In high school, I was a freshman when he was a senior and it was pretty rough. He was embarrassed by my constant shenanigans and as a result was pretty cold and demeaning at times. I shrugged it off as his problem, though, because naturally I thought I was a blast to be around. In secret, I really admired him. I thought he was supertalented musically, and I liked to play, too. For the first time, we had something in common, but we weren't able to get past our differences to actually enjoy playing together. We avoided each other until he graduated, and that was about it.

A few years later, when I was a freshman in college, I visited Brian at Vanderbilt right before Christmas break. My family was driving from Chicago to South Carolina and that was a good halfway point. Brian invited me to stay with him at his apartment, which was a total shock to me. We pretty much weren't speaking to each other at that point. But we partied together and I found that he had loosened up a bit and I had chilled out a bit and we discovered that we had a pretty similar sense of humor. Also, I chugged a beer faster than his roommate so I think that won him some bragging rights.

Ever since, we've grown closer every year. It's actually gotten to the point where I see him more than any other family member. It's never what I would have suspected growing up, but I'm so happy it's happened. He's now one of my best friends.

And then there's my oldest bro, David. He's probably the most empathetic and emotionally aware of the three of us. I would talk with him a lot when he was in college and we bonded over things we were passionate about. He was also supersupportive of me for as long as I can remember. I wish I saw him more, but being on opposite coasts and with him having a family and me doing the Hollywood thing, it just doesn't work out.

I was recently chatting with David on Facebook. We have a great rapport of picking up right where we left off and a great understanding of one another even though we aren't in constant communication. But I was a little sad/mad at myself when we started talking about his kids, because I didn't really know how old they were. I guess I'm kind of a bad uncle in that regard. I haven't sent them birthday presents . . . ever? I just don't think about it and then when I've missed it I feel guilty and then do nothing. Come to think of it, I don't even know *when* their birthdays are. I guess I owe them four and seven years of birthday presents, respectively. Or maybe it's five and eight. Maybe I should buy them some video games. . . .

Video games are how David and I have always bonded. I remember sitting on the floor of his bedroom watching him play games, trying to help with puzzles that he came across in the game play. I'm sure he didn't need my help, given that I was six years younger, but I really enjoyed the time spent with him. It made enough of an impression that I can still picture myself watching him play Megaman on some old tube TV. Nowadays David always wants me to get into one of the online games that he plays so that we can play together, but I don't really have the time to get sucked in. Then again, I spent hours playing Zelda by myself last summer, so I probably could play with Dave. As we write this book, I'm surprised at my automatic negative responses to new things sometimes. Especially since I like to believe that I am open and willing to try new things. Especially since I try to please others so much. Eugene's quest has inspired me, though. I will definitely make an effort to connect with my family at a deeper level. Luckily I'm not starting from *way* behind like he is.

What can you do to promote world peace?
Go home and love your family.

—*Mother Fucking Teresa*

Spilling the Family Tea

THE NIGHT AFTER our excursion at the mall is the grand finale: a large dinner planned for my grandmother's official birthday celebration. Before that, the clan descends upon my apartment for a light lunch and relaxation—well, less leisure, more frazzled organization on my end, with a couple of thoughtful surprises up my sleeve. I've decided to exempt Nos. 1–5 from this second exercise of extracting secrets because I'm already intimate enough with them. I'll focus my energies on my relatives from whom I could learn real, intriguing revelations, since none of them has had an opportunity in my many years on this earth to open up to me.

As relatives begin to populate my modest apartment, they mingle, fill up their plates with fruit, pastries, and eggs, and pull chairs around the couch in the living room to give the illusion that my grandmother is holding court. This presents a problem—by surrounding her, they've formed a ring, which for têtes-à-tête is practically impenetrable. I need to strategically separate each mark from the flock, but like a watering hole, when there's a bounty of assorted fruit platters, Asians will park their keisters for an interminable amount of time.

Then the first solution springs forth in my mind palace: the cake. I had personally ordered a specialty triple-berry birthday monstrosity and had a specific window of time to pick it up. I remember that nosy No. 6 had been on my ass about ensuring this was locked and loaded. She dug her own frosting-covered grave, and now is the time to make her lie in it.

I ask her to accompany me to retrieve it and the sheer force of her curiosity to see if I had somehow messed it up took her out of the circle and into my passenger seat. This might be the longest period I've ever been on-on-one with her in . . . my entire life? This realization strikes me as rather somber and irresponsible. How many of my family members have I only been familiarized with through group settings? How easy is it to consider someone flesh and blood and then only come in contact with them at a dinner table once every few years?

And then she says, unprompted, "Did you know your grandma's going to come live with me?"

A home run out of nowhere! My eyes widen, expression agog. My grandmother has lived here in Los Angeles ever since she immigrated decades ago to the United States—it was everyone's natural assumption that she would never relocate. Without going into much detail, out of respect for her privacy, all I can say is that this wasn't a flip decision. This was an enormous, stunning development: one that affects all of us and one I had zero inkling about.

"Who else knows?" I pry.

"Oh, well, your mom, your sisters, your uncles . . . most everyone, really."

Ouch. That stung a bit.

"Well what the hell, was anyone going to tell me?"

She looks me straight in the eye. "You're always so busy and hard to get a hold of. I wasn't sure if you really cared that much."

Double ouch. Leave it to No. 6 to tell it to me like it is. In learning the juiciest of secrets, I come away with two more shocking truths: By simply being present and engaged with another individual for a dedicated amount of time, I don't have to trick them into telling me something new—they'll instinctively volunteer it. And all this time, even as I've described my family's tumultuous history with intimacy and closed-offedness, I might be one of the worst perpetrators of all.

We return to my apartment to find that the crew has begun to disperse in preparation for the evening's festivities. By this point, I'm already exhausted. No. 7 is seated nearby, watching me quietly as I clean up.

She giggles. (I'm transcribing some of my relatives' broken English in a more direct way.) "You . . . clean . . . very, mm, not often, hmm?"

I shrug. "I don't like cleaning, but I'll do it for you."

She glances around my space, which I tried to make look as presentable as possible for their visit. "It's . . . more clean than last time."

"Thanks."

"You normally . . . very dirty." Laughs.

I laugh, too, because this isn't a lie. "Well, I've been trying to improve because I'm an adult now. Gotta grow up sometime."

She smiles and nods. I step out of myself for a moment, watching our small talk from the outside, and shut off the faucet. Dry my hands before placing them on my hips.

"I have a question," I say.

"Mmm?"

"Do you not like that I don't speak Korean?"

I don't know what came over me in that moment to open what could be a Pandora's box of cultural failures on my part as a Korean American who isn't fluent in the mother tongue, but I am suddenly compelled to ask the person in attendance whose English is the least developed.

She cocks her head slightly, considering her answer carefully. "I . . . think better you speak Korean, like your sister, because many times . . . I don't understand you."

I walk over, leaning against the chair diagonal from her. "Wait a minute. How much have you not understood when I talk to you in my life?"

She laughs. "Most . . . most of it."

I'm flabbergasted. Every comment or joke or discussion I've presented to No. 7 in more than thirty years could have completely gone over her head, and she never once brought it up or complained.

This is now the lowest point in my story. Realizing that someone you know and love has barely understood you for most of your existence is beyond sobering. It made me want to quit the English language altogether.

That night, as the coordinator in chief, I had to head to the restaurant at the InterContinental hotel downtown first to prepare the night's arrangements, but I also needed to make sure that everything was in place for my big secret that I planned to delight my family with. And by delight, I mean ambush.

The photos you see in this book, with some of the faces obscured, were taken at the hotel before and during my grandma's birthday dinner. If you know anything about elder Asians' relationships to getting their photos taken, you're aware that it's like asking someone to get their soul sucked out of their body by a demon. They absolutely despise it, and anytime I've even lifted my phone in a suggestive enough manner, my grandmother will literally duck and dodge out of the way as if the picture were a bullet.

Well, my deception this evening had twofold reasoning behind it: we needed photographic evidence for this book, and we had never gotten professional pictures taken as a family before. Kill two birds with one stone—as long as the old Asian birds don't fly away upon immediately seeing a camera lens aimed at them.

There, in the comfort of a suite, I snuck in my photographer to create an impromptu setup, and as everyone began to arrive, the creeping understanding of what was about to happen settled like a thick, fearful fog. I, the smug ringmaster, hammered home the inevitable: it's family portrait time, whether you like it or not.

To my surprise, some of the older relatives even appeared to be enjoying themselves as I coached them on how to pose like they're on the cover of *Vogue*.

As distant as I have proven to be as a conversationalist, I know my strengths as a partygoer, and I manage to liven up the proceedings like a clown pumping up the crowd at a circus.

Even Nos. 8 and 9, who have always been on the periphery, flank me with approving pats on the back as we watch my grandmother nervously get her solo portrait taken.

"Good job, Eugene!" No. 9 commends. "You'll have to send us the photos when they're done," No. 8 agrees.

"Aw, I'm glad y'all like this!" I heartily admit, my mood lightening.

"It's nice to have someone like you to bring this type of energy," No. 9 says. The bulb flashes. "Reminds me of my cousins."

I perk up, having forgotten that I still had to fulfill the challenge of procuring hot gossip from my targets. "Oh? I've never heard about them."

No. 9 was in the family via marriage, so her side was completely unknown to me. No. 8 pipes up, "Oh yeah, they were in the factory."

I grow instantly serious. "Oh no, they worked in a factory?" My immediate assumption was bleak, as most of my distant relatives were embroiled in some dark, bloody tale that spurred from the war-torn Korea peninsula.

No. 9 almost snorts. "No, not that factory. *The* Factory. You know, Andy Warhol?"

I blink. "What?"

She continues, "Yes, when you see pictures of the Factory, if you see a Korean person—that's probably your relative." She laughs. "They're really crazy, like you."

I blink again. "Are you freaking serious?"

This incredible revelation throws me for such a loop that I almost forget . . .

Ned. Fucking Ned. Jesus Christ, I forgot that I have to hug everyone. My night isn't over just yet—my greatest fear has yet to come.

Young and Restless

MY FAMILY DIDN'T just love and support me; they saved me. In 1997, I was diagnosed with clinical depression. Night after night, I would cry myself to sleep, telling my mother through tears that I was worthless, that I had no purpose in life. I was seven years old. Depression is something that can challenge the strongest of families, especially when exhibited by a young kid, and the strength they exhibit collectively has meant everything in forming my outlook toward life.

It's an insane thing for a kid of that age to experience these feelings and to think that about themselves, but depression doesn't contend with logic. These feelings stemmed from a place of looking at my peers and feeling different—specifically that they were talented and I wasn't, and that I in turn had nothing to offer to the world. Somehow I extrapolated this into the future and assumed that not standing out now meant that I would never have a place. This fear and anxiety consumed my every thought.

Repeatedly my parents would enter my room at night, alerted by my wailing. They tried their best to calm me, to tell me that kids don't have to worry about these things. I don't remember much from this time, but I do remember that they were always there. Unfortunately, it wasn't enough. My parents were left terrified that they had failed me, confused on how to help. I hit my lowest point when I admitted to my mother one night that I didn't want to live anymore.

My parents remained strong: they got me help via therapy, they supported my passions, and they guided me toward happiness. But it wasn't all smooth sailing from that point on. I have memories of lashing out at my parents, especially at my dad. Cursing, screaming, slamming doors. It's something my dad downplays and denies when I've tried to apologize as an adult. Maybe that's for the best. But I remember, and I live with the pain of those memories. Family is there to protect you from your own fears and mistakes, and by downplaying those memories he's offered me the chance to forget the pain and move on.

At a time when I wanted to give up, they worked double to fill my life with joy and structure. Eventually their positivity won out. And then . . . two years after getting diagnosed with depression, I nearly died in a car accident. Maybe you've noticed the scar I have underneath my neck. It's possible you haven't; cosmetically, it's about as ideal a placement as you could ever hope for as far as near-fatal lacerations go. My babysitter was driving and I had successfully talked my way into sitting in the front seat despite it being firmly against family rules. I've always been very persuasive. The accident was swift and mostly innocuous—a standard fender bender. Everyone else was fine, but I was too small to be in the front seat.

The airbag shot out at the speed of a bullet and thrust the edge of the seat belt deep into my neck, plunging it mere centimeters from my windpipe. I don't remember the accident, but I remember being put on the phone with my father as the paramedics lifted me from the front seat onto the stretcher and into the ambulance. My dad made it to the emergency room first. Throughout the entire surgery, he sat next to me, holding my hand, remaining strong. I needed a rock, and he was it. He never winced or looked away once. I can't imagine how difficult that was for him. Forty-five stitches later, he wasn't going anywhere.

My mom didn't make it to the hospital until the surgery had ended, trapped in the traffic caused by my accident. I'll always remember the image of her entering

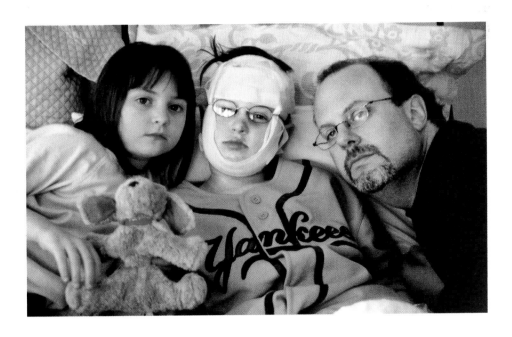

A BRIEF HISTORY OF TRYING

Author Henry David Thoreau was known for his philosophies of self-reliance, solitude, simple living, and independence, which he famously developed while living by himself for two years at Walden Pond. What he left out of his book was that he would often dip into town so that his *mom could do his fucking laundry.*

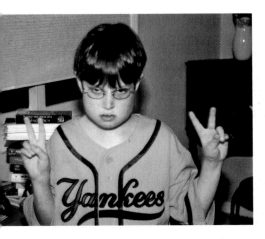

the doorway of my hospital room, a blurry figure standing at the foot of my bed and nearing closer. She broke into tears, stricken by grief and simultaneously overcome with the most extreme form of relief.

I was held out of school for a few months while I recovered, and once again they were rock stars, providing me strength in a time when I was at my weakest, aiding me through nightmares and painkillers. It's not easy to make recovery enjoyable, but my family did their best. My parents gave up their bed so I could spend my days bingeing movies and crushing episodes of *Judge Judy*. My sister gave me her favorite stuffed animal so I'd have someone to protect me from the bad dreams, and she provided live entertainment dancing at the foot of my bed—it was her turn to play Mr. Pillow Head. When I finally removed my bandages, we noticed my swollen face made me resemble Richard Nixon. It hurt to laugh, but it was nice to have something to smile about.

Ups and downs filled my childhood, but I consider myself lucky to no end to have the family I have. They stood by me at my lowest point, but what's more, they were there to offer warmth, humanity, and humor. I don't know who I would be without them, but I know who I am because of them. If my childhood taught me one thing, it's that life is fleeting and precious. Surround yourself with people you love, don't be afraid to laugh, and enjoy every moment of it. I'm thrilled to report that thanks to their love and guidance, I'm twenty years happy.

Hug Monster

FOR MY GRANDMOTHER'S big birthday dinner, we're in a very posh, private room seventy stories above downtown Los Angeles. The polished granite table is huge and circular, almost Arthurian, with my grandmother at the head—a reluctant queen.

I knew that I had a limited amount of time to strike on Ned's hugging prompt and that it would be hopeless to attempt it once the first course had arrived. Cursing his ooey-gooeyness in my head, I decide to embrace our failosophy and just go for it.

Go down your list, I encourage myself, knowing that starting easier might garner me the courage to get all the way down to No. 10. As everyone holds court, I stand and make my way over to No. 1, my little sister. I sheepishly open my arms and, with my voice lowered to a creaky whisper, I croak, "May I have a hug?"

She looks me over, eyebrow raised. "What did you say?"

I shush her. "Don't draw attention, because I don't want the others to know I have to do this. Just hug me."

She stands and obliges. "You used to do this all the time when we were kids, mainly because I was chubby," she mused as we held on to one another.

"Yeah, well you're not chubby anymore, so it's not as pleasant."

We laugh as I release her from my grasp.

No. 2, my older sister, had been next to us as this all transpired. She stands up dutifully and wraps me in her arms.

"I know this is for your book so let's get it over with."

I sigh. "Don't say that so loud, they're not supposed to know it's for the book."

"Well, maybe they'll actually do it, then, if they know you'll make money off it. Otherwise you're gonna look like a total weirdo."

My older sister and I hold on to each other, a sight for anyone who knew us growing up, since we didn't properly hug until we were both in college. Today it's not that awful, especially since we still find ways to make it riotous.

"Your boobs feel gross," I retort.

She lets go of me. "Thanks, your face is ugly."

Ah, family. Some things never change.

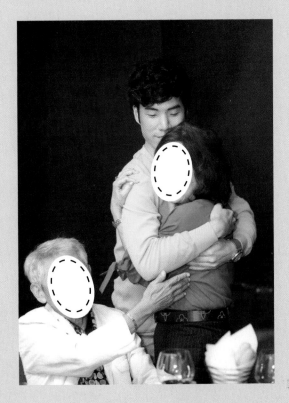

I have to traverse the room to approach No. 3, my mom. By the time I latch on to her, I know all bets are off for keeping this hug train covert, so I'll need to make this one count. She is, luckily, my easiest and longest hug.

"Sorry I don't call enough," I say. She pats me on the back.

"That's okay. I'm just glad we're here."

I can feel that she's smiling. I have to relax my grip to signal for her to let me go. The way she hugs me is as if it's the last time she'll ever get to do it, and I find myself almost getting choked up.

No. 4 is sweet and painless, since we've hugged before, but only in passing. Surprisingly, she's tickled pink by the gesture.

"You don't mind hugs?" I ask her as we embrace.

"No, I actually like them," she says.

"Huh, I wouldn't have thought that."

She sits back down. "Not liking hugs doesn't make you cooler, Eugene," she declares smartly.

I chart a path to No. 5, who's standing in a corner embroiled in a discussion, wineglass swirling in hand. For the life of me, I can't recall the last time I actually hugged him. If anything, we've definitely performed the "side hug" when seeing each other off with the manly double back pat for good measure. Embarrassed, I have to interrupt him in order to propose the question.

FAMILY

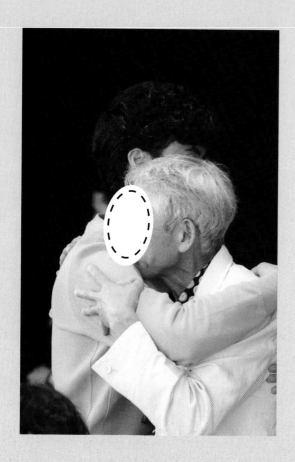

"Can . . . can I have a hug?"

I'm suddenly extremely self-conscious about the whole charade and feel more eyes in the room paying closer attention to my oddball demeanor. He considers my outstretched arms, momentarily perplexed.

"Are you leaving?"

I shake my head. "Nope, just . . . just want a hug, I guess."

He shrugs and yields. I feel the double back pat since, you know, we've still got to be masculine about it. But then, for several seconds, we hold each other, and he says something, almost at a whisper, so just only I could catch it:

"You do good."

Perhaps it was necessitated by the hug, but those three small words—whatever the hell they were supposed to mean—are a gratifying boost of esteem for me. After all, compliments are not readily distributed from all sides of my family, and in ways, my opening up through this try encouraged them to also bounce my challenges back at me in an affirmative way.

Now the hard part: the dreaded Nos. 6–10. No. 6, eagle-eyed as always, calls me out before I can even reach her.

"Whatever you're doing, it's weird."

I smile. "But I can have a hug, right?"

She snorts. "Sure, but I'm not standing up."

This type of hug I can relate to: fast, forced, and unusual for all parties involved. When I stand up straight, she slaps me lightly on the arm.

"Is this for a video?"

I pause. "No."

She squints at me. "Right."

I laugh internally, because there's no getting past my relatives when something is amiss. When I turn to No. 7, I take a moment to properly ask her for permission, and make sure that I come down to her seated level.

She authorizes my intimacy and I envelop her in a strong, substantial hug. I envision that I'm sending her all sorts of positive emotions through my palms, convinced that she must be deriving some sort of long-awaited enjoyment from this.

She very quickly pushes away from me with a defiant "Okay, that's enough."

I pull away, wondering how I can make her feel that I've taken exceptional care this evening. I gesture toward the cake I ordered—with the Korean word for grandmother (할머니) written in icing.

"Do you like the cake I got you?"

She takes a gander, very clearly noticing the Korean characters. A tiny smile. "Yes, I like . . . very much."

Obviously, No. 7 is my grandmother. I'll take whatever sign of approval she can spare and stride confidently to Nos. 8 and 9—both of whom I have never hugged before—but found the action to be far more straightforward than I could have ever imagined before this birthday weekend. They're both actually quite relaxed huggers, with No. 9 ending our clinch with a quippy "You are too funny." I can't tell if it's a compliment or an insult but I assume it's our particular brand of both-at-the-same-time.

Then I lock my sights on No. 10, who, quite literally, recoils as I descend upon him. He is viscerally on edge. Relating all too well to this unannounced invasion of personal space, I instead extend an open hand for a shake.

He deliberates over it for a few seconds before lifting his arm and presenting a closed fist.

"Fist bump."

I laugh out loud. You can bet your ass I've never even come close to hugging No. 10, but I have also never engaged in something as casual and brotherly as a fist bump. I close my hand and connect with him, knuckle to knuckle. I even burst my hand outward with a bomb sound effect.

"Explosion?"

He shakes his head. "No." And then he returns to his phone.

I managed to secure nine out of ten hugs—and one unforeseen fist bump—within the span of the bread course. More hugs achieved in less than half an hour than I had ever experienced with my family members in my entire lifetime.

Whatever the intended effect, my affectionate, albeit bizarre expressions of kindness had impacted every one of my relatives who had a seat at that table. The flow of conversation was open, easygoing, and real. Everyone had a fantastic time. And most important, my grandmother had a fitting ninetieth birthday,

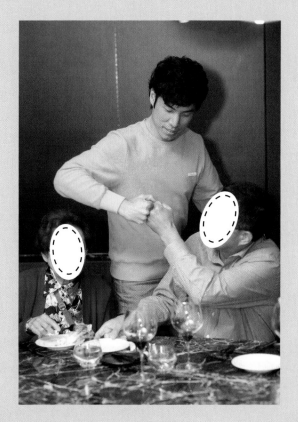

in part due to my once-in-a-lifetime preparedness in marshalling events, but more because, as she later told my mother, "I was just happy that everyone was there. That's all I needed."

It turns out, it's not just about "being there" for someone you love, although that is a huge part of the responsibility of maintaining healthy relationships with your friends and family—it's about committing to be truly present, which is a difficult, active mode to switch to when you've been flying on autopilot your entire life.

Keith's compliments challenge forced me to gaze beyond the surface assumptions I had of my loved ones and recognize what genuinely matters to them. Too often I've skated by like an acquaintance in my own home, communicating only what I knew to be canonical about our bonds without much digging deeper. By seeing past our ordinary repartee, I managed to make others feel truly seen and appreciated.

Zach's secrets challenge provided me not only with information I had never suspected of my relatives, but urgent actualizations about myself and how, sometimes, when you're in the dark about others' lives, that responsibility ultimately also falls on you to come into the light. Secretive behavior begets secretive behavior, and if I don't know something that everyone else is aware of, then I need to reexamine the ways in which I communicate.

Ned's hugging challenge was what most intimidated me at the advent of this entire try, but in retrospect, it was foolishly uncomplicated. To embrace someone you already consider family is not the insurmountable hurdle I built it up to be—it was breaking down the internal barriers that was actually most difficult.

Finally, the fact that I can entrust such a deeply confidential task—growing closer to my relatives—to my best friends is, in and of itself, a monumental try. In the beginning, I had turned my nose up, balking at their suggestions, searching for their devious intent to torture me. By the end, I concluded what is the most painful for me to concede: they were right, and I was wrong.

No matter how much pain, distance, or history informs the turbulent relations with your family and friends, know this: as small as these tries may have seemed, they are astronomical in their impact, because these are the relationships you have been conditioned to give up on the fastest, to believe they are a fixed, immovable point in your autobiography.

But it's these small, meaningful gestures that made my grandmother's birthday weekend and my try, even with its shortcomings, a massive success. Something as simple as a phone call, like the ones I'm about to make to my family members to check in after writing this sentence, can make you feel closer to them than you ever had allowed yourself to before.

When it comes to family, being there and being present are never a given condition, but something you have to work at. In other words, some tries are never finished.

WHAT WE LEARNED

✳ Keeping in touch is a two-way street. If you find yourself growing apart from a loved one, it may be on you to make the first move.

✳ There is no right way to parent. Your parents were just winging it, and if you have kids, you'll end up winging it, too. Anyone who raises a tiny human deserves all the credit in the world.

✳ As you embark on this journey of trying and failing, remember that no one has your back like family—however you define it. They're here for you. Use them for support and guidance.

✳ Most important, never underestimate the power of a hug.

Epilogue

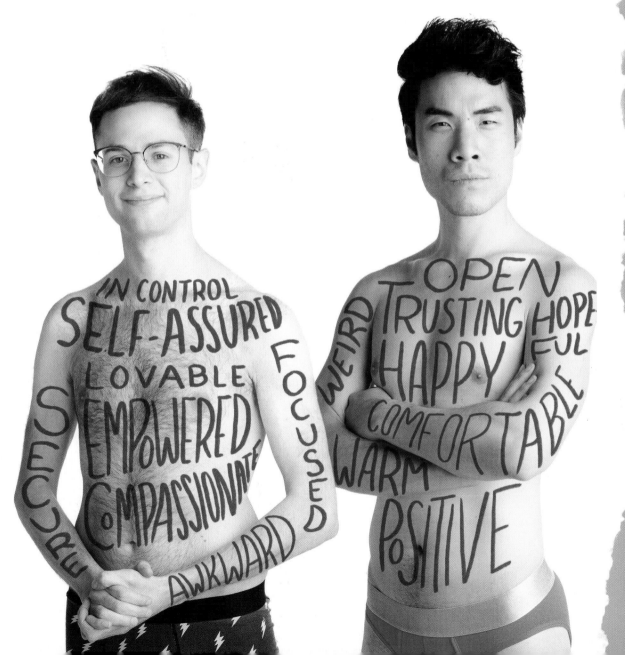

Y ou did it! You made it to the end! The first thing we want to say is *thank you*. We really poured our hearts and souls into writing this and we really appreciate that you read the whole thing. We hope that you came away knowing that we don't have all the answers; in fact *no one* has all the answers. It's okay to be clueless. I mean, we're like the poster children for cluelessness. But embracing what you don't know, what you don't like, what you can't understand, and what you're totally afraid of—*that's* where the magic happens. Stepping out of your comfort zone, failing, and flailing can be tough. Hell, it can be some of the most difficult things you ever do in your life. But when you come out the other side with the experience of having tried, of facing all your limitations and shortcomings, of falling flat on your ass—that's where the real growth begins. Now you're equipped with the confidence and knowledge and experience that wouldn't have been possible before. And that, friends, is the hidden power of fucking up.

About six months have passed since we first attempted the tries in this book. And in that time we've had a chance to truly consider the impact these attempts have had on our lives. As you know by now, failure is not a one-day thing, it's a lifestyle. So we wanted to take a minute to update you on how we've grown (and how we've regressed) . . .

YO. It's been a crazy few months. Where do I begin? Yesterday, I picked up a pair of jeans from the tailor because I had to get the waist taken in a couple inches. I'm now a 32. I've been a 34 waist since HIGH SCHOOL. That's fourteen years since I wore pants this size! My shirts are loose. My suits are loose. It's wild.

Please note that unlike the videos you see online of "amazing fitness and diet results in just thirty days!", all of this has been a really incremental process that comes with living my entire life differently. I didn't stick with the 100% vegan lifestyle. I did, however, adjust my diet to be only 15-20% meat, and I have really strived to limit my dairy intake. Becky and I make vegan recipes all the time, and we've found lots of delicious ways to make all-vegetable dishes. And get this—I haven't cooked a piece of meat in my house since I started this try six months ago! I've come a really long way.

But it definitely wasn't just a dietary overhaul. I have actually been working out 2–3 times a week for the past four months. Becky and I committed ourselves to waking up at 5:00 a.m. to take Orangetheory classes at 6. *I know.* I never thought I would live this way or be that guy, but it does make more sense to work out in the morning. I can still do everything I do in the day, and we just go to bed a little earlier.

Are there times when we fuck up and eat poorly? Yup. Vacation has become a "no rules" zone, but we make up for it when we get back home. Do we cancel workout classes the night before because we just aren't feeling up to it? Of course! But when we cancel one, we make sure to make the next one. We like the changes that we see and feel in our bodies. We're slimmer, yes, but really it's about being healthier.

You don't even realize how many other little problems in your life actually stem from your diet. By removing dairy, we found that we have fewer pimples. By cutting out meat, my issues with portion control aren't actually such a big deal. You can eat plants until you burst and be totally fine the next day!

I've always made excuses to avoid these changes in my life, and it was entirely out of fear. I was afraid to give up the tasty foods I loved. But they aren't out of my life, I just eat them less often, which makes me appreciate them more. I was afraid to feel weak in front of others, but now I see myself getting stronger with every workout. I feared this embarrassment, this loss, this change. But now I'm excited to continue forward on my health journey. Actually, it's not a health journey anymore. It's just my life. I've made it a habit. I'm really excited to continue leading this healthier life, and I'm going to look for other ways to keep improving.

I do want to add, though, that I didn't nail everything I set out to do in this book. I still don't talk to my family as much as I should. That's been a much harder bridge to cross. But for Christmas, I did book the family a big Airbnb so that all of the Habersbergers could share a roof for the holidays. It was ten people, one dog, and some really good times. Just like with my diet, you gotta start somewhere. Or at the very least, try.

FACING MY FASHION FEARS was really tough. There were moments where I felt uncomfortable every second of the day. I still sometimes dread getting dressed in the morning. But I got a lot of positive feedback! I realized that a lot of my fears were actually all in my head. I have started wearing jean jackets so much now to the point where I can't believe that I was ever afraid of them.

Even clothes shopping has gotten a little easier. Ariel and I went shopping for her birthday and it wasn't totally an awful, stressful experience anymore. It was actually kind of exciting. What new pieces might I find that were a little different, but still me? What could I find to push myself a little bit further? I ended up buying a pair of chunky black Cole Haan high-top boots—something that I would have imagined would be too intense for me before my try.

There are still days when I don't want to think about getting dressed and end up wearing sweatpants, but I try to think a little more about what shirt and shoes to pair *with* my sweatpants. Dare I say that I've tried to pull off athleisure a few times and have fucking nailed it? It feels weird to say *fuck*. I'm a dad now. Am I allowed to say fuck? I've tried to keep my sections of the book relatively clean, but it's in the fucking title of the book and now I'm just gratuitously saying fuck for the hell of it. See? Growth.

I'm still a little uncomfortable posing in photos, but I try to remember that it's just clothes. What I wear doesn't define me. I'm still goofy and silly while being smart and having ideas worth listening to. My clothing is just one potential expression of who I am. It's a representation of what I want to project on the outside. Fashion doesn't have to be a burden, it can be an opportunity to showcase the first impression of the man I want to be.

As for Wes, he's full-on crawling now and when he's holding onto my arms he can even pull himself up to a standing position. He actually said his first words the other day. They were "da bu gagu da traaaaaa," which sounds a lot like "The Hidden Power Of Fucking Up" so I think he's telling you to just go for it!

THE TRY GUYS is the best thing that's ever happened to me. Making these videos for the past few years has led me to evolve tremendously as a person, but if I've learned one thing through writing this book it's that the self is a constant work in progress. We really thought we'd pushed ourselves to the limit, but this book presented challenges deeper than we'd ever attempted before.

Maggie and I remain madly in love (awww) and my commitment to our relationship—to caring for her and caring for us—has proven to yield an important cornerstone of new life habits. I've become a more selfless boyfriend, constantly seeking ways to make her the center of my world. I've filled her life with loving gestures both big and small, from surprise weekend getaways and taking on remodeling our guest bedroom (with some help from my friends), to more everyday tasks like changing out the ugly light fixture in our living room (easier than I expected) and packing her the occasional to-go snack bag for work. I shifted the focal point of my universe and with everything I do I'm making sure she's the center of it.

Becoming a better boyfriend really entailed a journey into every chapter. While writing this book, I've experienced some setbacks with the medicine for my inflammatory disease, so I've been fitting in a full physical therapy routine before work. I volunteered to walk and feed our dog every morning to take some stress off Maggie. This routine provides an infusion of energy and good spirits into my mornings; the walk with Bowie serves almost as morning meditation, allowing me to wake up my brain and focus my mind before a busy day. The extra burst of energy allows me to be proactive about cleaning the dishes, tidying up around the house . . . you know, all the stuff I used to totally despise. Now instead of staring blankly ahead during my morning commute, I'm alert and awake, so I call my family and friends to catch up. I feel like I'm starting my mornings off right, which makes me more efficient at work, allowing for a work-life balance for probably the first time ever in my life. All this leads back to spending more time, and better time, with Maggie. Becoming a better boyfriend has really just been a journey of becoming a more fully realized *me*.

I'm not done growing. I don't think I ever will be. But I'm better now than I was when we started writing this book, just as I imagine I'll be better a year from today. The journey is bumpy, and it's okay to fuck up along the way, so long as your aim remains true. You've now got the tools to improve, and so do we. So here's to the future and becoming the most badass, empowered, confident, bizarre, cool, fucked-up versions of ourselves. Never stop having fun, don't be afraid to laugh at yourself, and above all, never stop trying.

I'D BE REMISS to reflect upon my attempts to grow more intimate with my family without mentioning how utterly resistant and uncomfortable they are with the idea of even being written about in this book. Moving the needle with my family is akin to moving mountains, and I honestly have no clue if I truly affected any change with my bold embrace of fucking up our clan's interpersonal dynamics.

However, the fact that I tried to create new inroads of communication with these people whom I know will be in my orbit for the rest of eternity is a testament unto itself, and the greatest lesson I could take from this experience. Many months later, we don't suddenly have a breezy rapport and a few days of forced social exercises didn't magically bring us closer together, but what I did manage to do was make everyone feel awkward and deeply distressed. Sure, for a few fleeting moments, we held each other in a fresh, radical regard, and that only came about with my decision to shake things up. But we have quickly settled back into our conventional ways. Still, I feel gratified that I was willing and able to challenge the status quo that has kept everyone in my family at arm's distance for years. In other words, I may have lost the war, but I did win a battle or two.

I will probably never become best buddies with No. 10, who would only give me a fist bump. In fact, he might like me less after my grand inquisition. But he knows me better than he ever has before and I have clearly tested his limitations. This is light years beyond where I stood with him prior to this endeavor; now we're not necessarily friends, but we're no longer complete strangers.

Having Keith, Ned, and Zach guide my family try was an impactful experience as well. After trusting their advice, I learned that when it comes to who you end up calling your friends, there are no random accidents. We were meant to be best friends, and I am dedicating myself to keeping it that way.

So many friend groups fall along the wayside as you grow older, and social circles morph and absorb and split themselves like amoeba. You and your friends owe it to yourselves to check in with one another and ensure that you not only have each other's backs, but that you can tell each other plain truths face-to-face, and sometimes test preconceived roles and notions. I followed Keith, Ned, and Zach's advice—something I don't do lightly—and emerged a more fully realized individual and friend because of it.

REMEMBER THE VERY FIRST PAGE OF THIS BOOK? When we were stranded on that raft for hours, with Keith's vomit chum attracting sharks? At the time, it was absolutely terrifying (and gross). But when we look back at it now, it was one of the best days in Try Guys history. Because we might have been miserable and scared—but at least we were together, as a family. And now we'd like to welcome you to the Try Guys family. Join us as the adventures continue, and know that we'll always have your back.

The ball is in your court. It's time to ask yourself the question, "What are you going to try?" You have the tools, you have the willpower, and you've got four best friends in us who can't wait to hear how it goes. Remember: since *failure is the goal*, it's basically impossible to mess this up. You're going in knowing it's not gonna go well. So pick something scary or crazy or fun! You got this, we promise.

As much as it pains us to say this, it's time to put the book down now. We know there's something in the back of your head that you've just been itching to try. *That's it. That's the one.*

Thank you for coming on this journey with us four fuck-ups. And welcome to the club.

Acknowledgments

In all of our tries, we start from a place of not knowing much. Only through the guidance of the amazing people we work with do we end up creating really awesome stuff. This book is no exception, and there are many people to whom we want to express tremendous gratitude.

We'd like to start by thanking Aaron Karo, our fifth writer on this project. Being tasked with the incredible challenge of helping the four of us create a uniform tone and execution, while still enabling all of our personal stories and voices to shine through is no small feat. He also bugged us just the right amount to keep us on our deadlines. Even we need a good kick in the pants sometimes.

A barrage of thanks is also in order for Jessica Felleman, our literary agent, for helping us realize the vision of our first book. From our first meeting in a coffee shop in LA we knew we were in good hands. She made the process of creating and pitching to publishers both painless and exciting, and we can't imagine a better person to have on our side.

To Matthew Daddona, our editor, and all the amazing people at Dey Street, including Carrie Thornton, Lynn Grady, Andrea Molitor, Nyamekye Waliyaya, Kell Wilson, Imani Gary, Julie Paulauski, Gena Lanzi, Kelly Rudolph, Heidi Richter, T. Pitoniak, Caitlin Garing, Josh Marwell, Carolyn Bodkin, and Mumtaz Mustafa. And to Michelle Crowe, who tackled designing this book with gusto and brought the pages to life, resulting in the colorful and energetic spreads you've just finished enjoying. We are so grateful to have a team that can bring our vision to life. Matthew's enthusiasm from the beginning helped us to know that what we were writing mattered, and that people could truly benefit from it. Additionally, every time we walked into HarperCollins we were met with such kind, enthusiastic people who believed in us and our book. It's like having a little set of excited cousins who live solely in a building in lower Manhattan.

To all of the Foundry team, including Sara DeNobrega, Mike Nardullo, Alex Rice, Sarah Lewis, and Claire Harris, who handle the business side of making and selling a book. We had no idea what we were doing, and we owe you our unending thanks and praise. You're our other cousins in Manhattan. Our family reunion is gonna be lit.

To our wives and significant others, Ariel, Becky, Maggie, and Matt, we owe everlasting gratitude. Their encouragement and understanding of our ridiculous lives deserve daily thanks and appreciation, of which we are always behind on. They are frequently burdened by the weirdness of our work, doubly so when we decide to write about them, and their acceptance means the world. They fill our lives with joy, purpose, and meaning. We love you. In fact, all of us love all of you, which may be kind of weird.

To our families—the Fulmers (Susan, Jim, Grace), the Habersbergers (Patricia, Donald, David, Brian), the Kornfelds (Adam, Margo, Stephanie), and the Yangs, Kims, and Chos (Min, Jae, Mr. Cho, Christie, Whitney, and most especially, 할머니)— who raised us to be the people we are. Who allowed us to fail. Who encouraged us to take risks. Who made mistakes themselves that could allow us to see that nobody is perfect. Who show us love and compassion and whose lives are now less private because of us. We thank you (and also apologize for, you know, the weird stuff).

To Wes, who was born and lived the entire first year of his life throughout the founding of our new company and the writing of this book. May you try many new things in your life and never be afraid to fail. We're sorry we said "fuck" a lot. You will always be loved by your father, your mother, and your three Try Uncles. To our collective future children, we love you too, but you weren't born yet when we wrote this so you're just going to have to deal with not getting a direct shoutout.

To our incredible staff at 2nd Try, LLC: Rachel, Devlin, Miles, Kasiemobi, YB, Alexandria, Will, Elliot, Nick, and Allison, you enable us to tackle so many projects while maintaining incredible quality in all that we do. We admire everyone's commitment to what we're growing and can't wait to continue making more amazing stuff together. You are all so valuable to our sanity and you have helped elevate our content to new levels. We can't thank you enough for lending us your talents and skills.

And last, but in no way least, we want to thank our fans. This book is for you, but this book is also because of you. Never in a million years did we think that we'd be living such fruitful, exciting lives. It is because of you that we have been shaped into such worldly people. And it continues to be because of you that we motivate ourselves to keep going. All the sleepless nights, all the risks we take, they are all worth it because we know we have an incredible community of loving people waiting to see what we do next. We hope you get as much out of this book as we have, and we can't wait to make the next great thing for (and because of) you.

About the Guys

THE TRY GUYS—Keith Habersberger, Ned Fulmer, Zach Kornfeld, and Eugene Lee Yang—are video producers with a willingness to try just about any-thing. Their videos are dedicated to exploring people's passions and identities in an effort to better understand the world around them. They're known for pos-sessing a keen understanding of and passion for the viral video landscape, and for creating positive, comedic, and impactful content with an eye for repeatable formats and shows. Their online comedy docu-series has garnered over two bil-lion views to date, with their YouTube channel gaining over five million subscribers within the first six months of its inception. In early 2018, they founded 2nd Try, LLC, an independent production company that aims to bridge the gap between digital and traditional media. In October of 2018, the group took home the top honor of Show of the Year at The Streamy Awards, where they also served as hosts. They are based in Los Angeles. You can follow their work on Youtube or at TryGuys.com.

HarperCollins books may be purchased for educational, business, or sales promotional use. For information, please email the Special Markets Department at SPsales@harpercollins.com.

FIRST EDITION

Designed by Michelle Crowe

Cover and chapter heading photos by JD Renes

Chapter heading illustrations, bobble head illustrations, other color illustrations throughout, and creative by Jack Sjogren

Other graphics throughout (ripped paper, masking tape, speech bubbles, book doodles, brain illustration) by OoddySmile Studio / Shutterstock, Inc., jocic / Shutterstock, Inc., strogaya / Shutterstock, Inc., Natasha Pankina / Shutterstock, Inc., shopplaywood / Shutterstock, Inc.

Author photo (online) by Mandee Johnson Photography

Library of Congress Cataloging-in-Publication Data has been applied for.

ISBN 978-0-06-287961-5

19 20 21 22 23   10 9 8 7 6 5 4 3 2 1